CW00337454

INJURED PARTIES

INJURED PARTIES

Solving the Murder of Dr Helen Davidson

Monica Weller

The History Press

Cover Illustration: Joop Snijder Photography/Shutterstock

First published 2016

The History Press
The Mill, Brimscombe Port
Stroud, Gloucestershire, GL5 2QG
www.thehistorypress.co.uk

British Library Cataloguing in Publication Data.
A catalogue record for this book is available from the British Library.

ISBN 978 0 7509 6695 5

Typesetting and origination by The History Press
Printed and bound by CPI Group (UK) Ltd.

Contents

Acknowledgements

First and foremost I wish to thank Maria Marston for being so trusting when she directed me to the story about Dr Helen Davidson's unsolved murder. *Injured Parties* owes much to Maria and to her parents, Bob and Fennis Marston.

I am indebted to many people in and around the Buckinghamshire town of Amersham, who have tirelessly encouraged me to complete this book. To Barbara Webber, an Amersham lady, who ended her career as head of Physiotherapy at the Royal Brompton Hospital and, in retirement, is heavily involved with Amersham Museum where she has had many roles ranging from secretary, cataloguer of photographs, guided walks organiser, to general factotum. Thank you, Barbara for your generosity of time, thoughtfulness, support and for your introductions to many local people who were able to help me. Thanks to Barbara's friend Natalie Ross, another Amersham lady whose family were patients of Dr Helen Davidson, who has always wanted closure on the matter of Dr Davidson's tragic death, and whose information about people and places in the town regularly filled my email inbox during the course of my research.

I would like to give a special thank you to medical journalist Tim Albert. From the start of my research he pointed me in the direction of the British Medical Association and the *British Medical Journal* and I never looked back. More generally, I am grateful to archivists and librarians at The Royal College of Anaesthetists, The Royal Society of Medicine, The Royal College of General Practitioners and St John Ambulance.

In the early stages of my research I visited Professor David Bowen, the forensic pathologist who carried out the post-mortem on the body of Dr Helen Davidson in 1966. I am very grateful for the time he took to share his knowledge and material with me, and for introducing me to the world of the forensic pathologist. For help on specific medical queries my thanks go to Dr Margaret Chilton, Dr Rhona Maclean, Professor Neil McIntyre, Dr Wendy Kelsey and Dr Brenda Sanderson. A huge thanks also to the following: Dr David Howell, Mrs Rosemary Howell, Dr Bryn Neal, Dr Keith Heywood, Mrs Barbara Ogden and Mrs Pauline Argles. And a special thank you to Wright Funeral Directors, for filling in vital details about procedures on 10 November 1966.

I am indebted to Mrs Janice Still, a retired chartered Biomedical scientist, fellow of the Institute for Biomedical Science, a magistrate on the High Wycombe bench, and a former chairman of the Friends of Hodgemoor Wood, for her in-depth knowledge of the wood.

Thank you to the following people for their intimate knowledge about people and places in Amersham, its villages close by and Hodgemoor Wood; I know there are many who have waited patiently as I attempted to uncover the facts. To Pam Appleby MBE, a former chairman of Amersham District

Council, who also served as a magistrate on the Amersham Bench, and was a patient of Dr Davidson for over twenty years. Dennis Silcocks who is the former headmaster of Hyde Heath Infant School, Janet Bangay, Ann Honour, Irma Dolphin, David Oxley, Ruth Groves, Derek Swains, Mary Grove, Joyce and Hilary King, Wendy Stevens, Rob and Suzette Stevens, Pat Drew, Michael Baughan, Vera Herriott, Mary Knight, David Mulkern, Pauline Willes, Carol Bain, Barbara Cox, Rosie Woodfall, Elizabeth Sainsbury, Catherine Morton, Trevor Richardson, Rosalind Pearce, Betty Waters, Daphne Lytton, Edward Hance, Mike Brookes, Michael Larcombe, Elizabeth Small, Vaughan Ward, Stephanie Lee, Pat Smith and Pam Joiner.

For help on police matters, thank you to the following: New Scotland Yard, Thames Valley Police, Ms Sara Thornton QPM the Chief Constable of Thames Valley Police, Susan Farmer in the Homicide and Serious Crime Command of the Metropolitan Police, Peter Beirne of the Major Crime Investigations Review Team at Thames Valley Police, the Association of Chief Police Officers (ACPO), National Association of Retired Police Officers (NARPO), Tony Dale, Brian Shirley, Charles Farquhar, former police photographer John Bailey, Jo Millington BSc of Manlove Forensics Ltd, John Young, Daphne Browne, Janet Greenland and Roger Reynolds.

Thank you to archivists and librarians at the following organisations and associations: the Royal Free Hospital Archives whose collection was largely transferred to the City of London, London Metropolitan Archives in 2014. Putney High School, Sherborne Old Girls, Surrey History Centre, Amersham Museum, Chiltern Medical Society, Friends of Hodgemoor Wood, Buckinghamshire County Council, Sherborne Local Studies, Cornish Records Office, Cornish

Studies Library, Croydon Library, Bristol Reference Library, Chesham Library, Amersham Library, Janice Talmer, Nick Hide of the Clan Davidson Association, Hanslope History Society, Wimbledon Museum, London Transport Museum, The Amersham Society, Charterhouse School, National Museums of Liverpool, Lee Manor Society and David Plumer, HM Courts and Tribunal Service, Forensic Science Society, the Army School of Education and the Forestry Commission. To Judy Cardnell at Colfe's School, Adam Green, assistant archivist at Trinity College Library, Cambridge, the Centre for Kentish Studies, Royal Bank of Scotland Group Archives, The National Archives, Chilterns Forest Office, Reading Borough Libraries, Imperial War Museum, British Library, City of Westminster Archives Centre, Dorset History Centre, Institution of Mechanical Engineers, Wandsworth Heritage Service, BT Group Archives, Oxford County Council, Wimbledon Museum of Local History, Merton Historical Society, Croydon Local Studies Library, Friends of East Peckham School. And to Rob Hume and Tim Webb of the RSPB who were able to add to my knowledge of bird-watching in Hodgemoor Wood.

Thank you to Ordnance Survey, G.I. Barnett and Son Ltd, and to Theo De Bray and John Moxon for their expert knowledge about maps. Thank you to the newspapers, editors of publications, online forums, reporters and press photographers that have helped me in many ways: *The Cornishman, Cornish Guardian, West Briton*, Rebecca Leon of Bois Own community newsletter for Chesham Bois, *Oxford Mail, Buckinghamshire Advertiser, Buckinghamshire Examiner, The Bucks Herald, Bucks Free Press, Wiltshire Times, The Times* Digital Archive, Newsquest Oxfordshire, *NARPO News* and *Sword Magazine*. Special thanks to Mike Dewey for delving into the archives at the *Bucks Free Press*, also to Malcolm Wade, and to Ron Haddock. The following online resource websites provided me with valuable leads: Amersham News, Views and Information, the Hyde Heath website and RootsChat.

I must also thank the following: Martin Rolf, Reggie Revel, Peter Cook, Richard Anderton, Rena Hume, George Wright, Father Denis Lloyd, John Fox, David and Margaret Larcombe, Felicity and Sophie Garrett, Jocelyn Osborne, Stephen Pratt of B&M Motors in Amersham, Jeremy Preston, Lindy Fleetwood, Michael McDonnell, Tonbridge Parish church, Pat Mortlock, the superintendent of Chiltern Crematorium, Bucks Fire and Rescue Service, Peter Worlidge, Brian Duffey, Vince Latter, Peter Dodgson, Sheila Broomfield, Rosemary Tandy, Enid Hounsell, Ken Rogers, Jennifer Statham, Christine Askew, Maureen Giles, Sherrill Robertson Bland and Maurice Blisson.

To the London Transport enthusiasts who have helped me with their knowledge of buses, bus garages and in particular the London Transport Country Bus network, a huge thank you. Especially Richard Proctor, who has had an interest in Amersham's buses since childhood, and Jonathan Wilkins, who is not alone in his memories of the London Transport bus that had served the capital and its surrounding countryside for a generation. To Bill Harvey MBE, Audrey Gossedge, Uxbridge Bus Garage, Mary Adlington, Mike Beamish, Robin Reynolds and Sydney Adams.

I would like to thank everyone at The History Press whose faith in *Injured Parties* means so much to me. For his advice and support, huge thanks to my agent Robert Smith who quietly encouraged me, questioned, edited the manuscript and believed in my story. And to my partner John, who put up with this sleuth during her seven years of research and writing, thank you.

Foreword

On 26 June 2013 it was reported in *Get Reading*, the Berkshire online publication, that Thames Valley Police had forty-two unsolved murders on its files. Despite a thorough search I was unable to find a list of victims and dates of their murders. I therefore emailed Peter Beirne of the Major Crime Investigations Review Team at Thames Valley Police whose remit is to review and reinvestigate unresolved homicides. Beirne sent me a list of the cases from 1958 through to 2014, pointing out it is not meant to be definitive as it is continuously under review. The document also stated the crimes, being unsolved, are open investigations and therefore no further information will be released. In an email to me Beirne wrote:

> You may not be aware but we were successful in convicting the killer of another 1966 offence back in 2012 [he knew of my literary involvement in the murder that year of Dr Helen Davidson]. That was the murder of a young

girl called Yolande Waddington in Beenham near Newbury
[Berkshire] and the offence occurred the month before
Dr Davidson's death.

David Burgess was jailed in 2012 for the murder of Yolande
Waddington half a century ago, after modern forensic techniques helped prove his guilt. Bloodstains on items still available
from the murder scene were reinvestigated. On 20 July 2012,
BBC News Berkshire asked: 'Why, despite blood from Burgess
being found at the scene, did it take police more than four
decades to bring him to justice? When asked whether mistakes
were made in the original inquiry, Peter Beirne, head of the
Thames Valley Major Crime Review team, answers a defiant
"no".' *Get Reading*, on the same date, reported that Thames
Valley Police, who have a dedicated team of detectives and
staff, were committed to reviewing and reinvestigating
unsolved crimes. A Thames Valley Police spokesperson said,
'The passage of time is no defence and review teams across the
country are carrying out such work daily to ensure our com-
munities are protected.'

In a letter to me, the Chief Constable of Thames Valley
Police, Ms Sara Thornton, wrote: 'Because the case [of Dr
Helen Davidson's murder] is part of a cold case review they
are not able to disclose information regarding the case.' She
added, 'In any request of this nature we have to ask, "How will
the disclosure of this information assist in the investigation
balanced against any distress that the publication may cause
any living relations or friends of the victim?".'

In the case of Dr Davidson's murder, despite being fifty
years ago, the problem of writing about this unsolved case has
brought challenges. There were last-minute hurdles to cross
prior to publication. One of my main contributors, having

made amendments to the manuscript about his memories and comments surrounding the case, withdrew further assistance. But his earlier help was invaluable and did enable me to investigate the case further and to reach my own conclusion about the unsolved murder.

For legal reasons, some names have had to be changed, some characters must remain unidentifiable, information cannot be attributed to main sources, and sometimes these sources have to be deleted from the story. Identities have to be protected to avoid possible repercussions. However, the story remains true. Seven years have passed since I began writing it. Some people who helped with my investigation have passed away and the case of Dr Davidson's murder has slipped further into insignificance. But I want to keep this story alive. I want readers to feel what I was up against in my search for the truth.

Prologue:
1 May 1967

At around 11 a.m. on Monday morning, Donn Small, the 44-year-old district officer for the Forestry Commission's branch office in the small Buckinghamshire town of Princes Risborough, sat in his office alone at his desk with a mug of coffee, reading through the morning post. He had been copied in to the latest correspondence between his Forestry Commission boss and the police. One letter dated 27 April 1967, from the Forestry Commission in Cambridge to the inspector in charge at Buckinghamshire County Police, Amersham police station, read:

Dear Sir

During the summer of 1966 the Commission's clearing and replanting operations at Hodgemoor Wood were suspended pending reconsideration of the future management plan for this woodland. Subsequently, Dr Davidson's body was discovered in the wood. The Commission's revised management proposals have now been approved and I am ready to make preparations for a resumption of work. Would you please advise on whether your authority has any objection or comment to make in relation to resumption of our operations in any part of this woodland?

Yours faithfully
for Conservator

The second letter was from Supt Aubrey Smith of Buckinghamshire Constabulary in reply to the Forestry Commission's letter of 27 April:

Dear Sir

Hodgemoor Wood

Thank you for your letter of the 27th regarding the above. As far as police are concerned there is no objection to the Commission continuing with their operations at Hodgemoor. We feel that it is unlikely that anything will be found in the wood which will help with enquiries. However should any of your staff find anything which may be interesting perhaps you would let me know. In the meantime may I take this opportunity of thanking you for your co-operation and help in this enquiry.

Yours faithfully

Small laid the letters to one side and picked up a large lever-arch file labelled Hodgemoor Wood. It was bulging with bundles of carbon copies of letters from Forestry Commission departments, solicitors, MPs, complaints from private individuals, parish council minutes, official documents penned in the margins with further notes about the future of Hodgemoor Wood, and maps, lists of trees and shrubs. They all dated back to 6 September 1966, when the troubles came to a head, and presented a picture of a woodland war.

Storms of protest had raged over the previous three years as furious local residents, determined to preserve the ancient hardwood plantation of Hodgemoor as an amenity, watched thousands of beech trees close to Hodgemoor being felled by the Forestry Commission and planted with regimented rows of conifers. The Commission was equally as determined to replace depleted stocks of wood following the Second World War with acres of quick growing softwoods for commercial cropping and profit. When this is over, Small thought, this endless paperwork will be preserved in official government files and not see the light of day for years. But it wasn't over yet.

Small, who had been with the Commission in Princes Risborough since 1963, was devoted to his work, and had to take charge of and administer new unpleasant government policies to make profit from the woodlands in Buckinghamshire. He was regarded as someone who would tread on people's toes to achieve his goals. The as yet unsolved murder of Dr Davidson six months earlier in Hodgemoor Wood just thirteen miles from his office was all he needed: a manhunt in the area and another interruption to the Forestry Commission's commercial activities. It was a crime that even amateur sleuths in the area were trying to solve, but couldn't. Someone in years to come, he mused, *will* see the wood for the trees. He took a pen, wrote 'Davidson, Murder Investigation, for filing' across the top of each letter, signed and placed them on top of the Hodgemoor Wood file in his in tray.

Naturally, Small had been taking an intense professional interest in the murder on his patch of the county since reading the dramatic headlines in the *Buckinghamshire Advertiser* on 17 November 1966: 'KILLER BEHIND SOMEONE'S DOOR. Police hunt psychopath for Dr Davidson's murder. Full scale manhunt is being organised in Bucks this week following the discovery in Hodgemoor Wood near Chalfont St Giles of the brutally battered body of Dr Helen Davidson.' Small could still visualise the photograph of the murdered woman on the front page, lying on her back on a bed of autumn leaves. The photograph had been deliberately cropped to save unnecessary suffering to her family and showed just her legs and the faithful wire-haired terrier sitting next to his mistress.

Sometime around New Year, two months after the murder, he'd begun to hear rumours circulating around the office about a length of charred wood from a bonfire or charcoal kiln, alleged to be the murder weapon. Scientific tests, according to the rumour, had shown it was poplar wood. This concerned Small. Oddly enough, nothing in press reports that had previously filled local newspapers and national media for weeks had even hinted at a length of wood from a poplar tree. In fact, initially it was reported that the doctor had been struck across the head by a heavy metal weapon. The theory that subsequently dominated news reports was that the killer used a lump of wood found close to the scene of the crime to slay his victim. But, he asked himself, where had the rumour about the poplar come from? He had spoken to the police about his doubts of course. Even though he thought he may be of some use to the police authority, being an expert on all aspects of trees, timber research and the management of large areas of forest, they didn't invite him to view the length of poplar wood which was, in their words, 'part of a murder investigation and which had been carefully retained as an exhibit'.

Nor were the police interested in what he had to say. He told them it was unlikely in his opinion that the poplar wood, of the species they were describing, actually came from Hodgemoor. It wasn't native to the woods. To the layman this unmistakable, tall slim tree grows very big, very fast in rows around the edges of agricultural fields to protect against wind erosion and gives off millions of dandelion-like clock seeds in the spring, and on which mistletoe grows easily. It is not the type of tree you see in Hodgemoor's woodland. But the police weren't impressed. With the description of that entire woodland etched on his mind, he explained to them that the 282 acres of woodland, which had been leased three years earlier by the Forestry Commission from Buckinghamshire County Council for the next 150 years, had been meticulously documented. It was one of the largest remaining tracts of broad-leaved deciduous woodland in the Buckinghamshire Chilterns, made up of oak standards, beech, sweet chestnut, hornbeam, ash, hazel, birch, dense thorn, scrub and bracken. But not poplar. It was also impenetrable and unproductive as woodland. Small got the feeling that his opinion didn't fit the police theory about the chance killing in which the supposed attacker picked up the length of wood, which they said had been felled and burnt close by and just happened to be lying around close to the crime scene. They couldn't see what was obvious to Small: that the poplar had to have been taken to the woods and its origins could be significant in a murder investigation. The police had been prepared to take things at face value. Or they didn't want to probe.

The bonfires the police talked about puzzled him. The High Court injunction served on the Forestry Commission and Buckinghamshire County Council over two months before the doctor's murder had halted tree felling and banned bonfires. It seemed somebody who didn't know about the court order was making them illegally. As far as Small was concerned the police findings were sinister. It was as if they were modifying the facts to fit their theory. What did the police have to gain?

He sat at his desk, elbows resting in front of him, head cupped in his hands, thinking. He looked up and stared through the metal-framed window that gave on to extensive fields tightly packed with rows of experimental, metre-high, sawn-timber stakes simulating fence posting. Beyond the surreal scene of wood soaked in creosote being tested for rot, winding around the distant woodland on the fringes of the security-fenced compound, was a collection of drab, flat-roofed buildings erected for the army during the Second World War. They were now home to the scientific community of the Forest Products Research Laboratory, part of the government's Ministry of Technology. Scientists, barely aware of the commercial world outside their own, planned the future for moneymaking timber projects.

Small reminded himself he was under pressure to turn the grim woodland at Hodgemoor into a profitable enterprise. Harvesting and marketing is the remit now, not just conservation and wildlife reserves. And they could do without the intrusion of the angry protest group calling itself the Hodgemoor Woods Association under the leadership of a Mr Haylett, which consisted of delegates from local amenity societies, members of local parish councils and the rural district council, who all saw the forest only as a place for picnics, walking their dogs and riding their horses. Small was on his theoretical podium.

They don't appreciate that unless scrubland is cleared, Hodgemoor won't provide either the easy access or enjoyment they're demanding. I've never seen more than a dozen or so out of the hundreds of people who supposedly spend time there. Why do they only complain now that the woods are to be put in order and made pleasant and usable? Private woodland owners look to the Forestry Commission in the Chilterns for active support in converting the great Chiltern concentration of unproductive beech woods into a profitable enterprise. We know woodlands like Hodgemoor provide peace to some members of the public, but if it is left in its present state it won't provide enjoyment or a contribution towards our great national effort in woodland improvement to make money.

All said and done it is an area of outstanding natural beauty and there will have to be compromises. The Forestry Commission will probably need to lean more heavily in the direction of management for amenity. Maybe this controversial government edict of management for profit is a pipe dream.

His thoughts drifted back to Dr Davidson. It was an ideal place to carry out a murder. He picked up the file and leafed through it for a map showing the exact location of the body. He stared down at the pastel-coloured drawing. A body could have lain there in the dense wood for at least a day and not be discovered, which is exactly what had happened. Small did not know the ins and outs of a murder inquiry but was not impressed with what he'd read in the Buckinghamshire newspapers. What hope was there now six months after the crime, and, no doubt, the police investigation petering out, of finding uncontaminated evidence? Who, amongst those police officers involved, knew anything about this woodland or about the effect of the injunction? The puzzle about the poplar fascinated Small. Why had it not been mentioned in police reports in the newspapers? There was something misleading about it.

For six months the murder had dumbfounded the police. They were still no closer to solving it. Someone, thought Small, will eventually dig into old Forestry Commission files, retrieve paperwork spanning the time of the doctor's murder and apply their logic to the unsolved crime. Someone will see that the police story about the poplar wood was an unhelpful diversion in a murder hunt.

I

Dr Helen Davidson:
A Woman of Habit

Dr Davidson made an impression on all of her patients. In the sleepy yet sophisticated market town of Amersham in Buckinghamshire, where she had practised as a GP since the last days of the Second World War, they described her as a highly respected doctor who visited her patients because she wanted to, not because she had to. Patients still recall every detail of this well-to-do, independent lady, married to her profession: every mannerism, her caring nature and the way she walked with a vigorous stride as if on a mission. They remember her heather-mixture tweed suits in a neutral or otherwise unremarkable colour, and the brooch in her lapel. One patient remembers how she drove her good-looking but not upmarket Hillman Minx saloon like a Porsche to reach sick patients quickly, and another how she did not drive it without her finest kid- or sheepskin-lined suede gloves which were part of her. Her hair cut in military style made her look older, not very feminine and distinctly un-Swinging Sixties. Another patient remembers her emerging from her consulting room into the surgery's waiting room as cool as a cucumber, having dealt with somebody noisy with a grievance. None of her patients could think of Dr Davidson in terms other than being a wonderful doctor. She was, as far as some were concerned, nothing less than a god.

The announcement in *The Times* on 1 August 1961 of Helen's forthcoming marriage to Herbert Baker therefore came as a surprise to everyone. The wedding took place the following month on 22 September at St Mary's church in Wimbledon. Helen was almost 45 and retained her maiden name after the marriage. Herbert, a widower, was thirty-one years her senior and had succeeded in wooing this definitely not-the-marrying-type lady. Uncharacteristically for such a private person, her family life and background being strictly private, late that summer Helen confided in a long-standing patient, Mrs Vera Herriott, about her imminent marriage. Herbert it seems was pushing Helen, saying marriage would be better for her, rather than coming home to an empty house each day, and that she could still do her birdwatching. 'Dr Davidson told me the one thing in her life, other than her work, was birdwatching and going out for long, solitary walks in woodland with her dog. She admitted she didn't think she'd ever get married, she had kept clear of all emotional attachments and it never interested her,' said Mrs Herriott. It was a time when for most professional women, it was still a clear case of either a career or marriage, not both. This was the only occasion Dr Davidson discussed her personal affairs with Mrs Herriott.

Herbert Baker was something of a mystery. In the tight-knit Buckinghamshire village community of Chesham Bois, which lies halfway between Amersham and Chesham, and where the doctor had lived since 1954, some locals knew she had married but never consciously heard the name of her husband, let alone knew his face. Some referred to him as a little old man with white hair, frail-looking, a most unattractive man, or as that old boy who walked with a stoop. Even the doctor's neighbours in the adjoining semi only vaguely remember the doctor's modern blue car and Mr Baker's old black one but were not aware of any comings or goings. The couple were rarely seen out together other than in the early 1960s at the occasional choir practice at Amersham Choral Society. Michael Baughan, a local builder who'd had a run-in one Sunday morning with Herbert for rotovating his front garden in the nearby village of Hyde Heath, said, 'He was objectionable ... the last person anyone would want to marry and started preaching about working on the Sabbath. He said it was the Lord's Day, the day of rest, and how we have six days to work and what I was doing was against God's Law.' It was Baughan's one and only encounter with Herbert Baker, the elderly man who had grown up in a different era with a strict code of ethics – the difference between right and wrong had been drummed into him. It seemed few in and around Amersham, though, had a good word for him.

According to local magistrate Pam Appleby, the marriage was a disaster, not a happy one. 'Rumours circulated round Old Amersham that Herbert had persisted in a relationship with his housekeeper of thirty years, Kathleen Cook, since his marriage to Helen,' said Pam:

When Herbert's first wife Ruby died the housekeeper thought she'd be in with a chance. He spent half his days back in his previous house in Hyde Heath, which he had assigned to the housekeeper, while Helen was working. I seem to recall there was a problem. Helen was not a pretty woman but when she smiled her face lit up and that after her marriage in 1961 the light went out of her wonderful blue eyes. She lost her smile and sparkle.

Wednesday 9 November 1966

It was Wednesday, her afternoon off, but the day started like any other day for Dr Davidson. Whether it was summer or winter, light or dark, she was out soon after 6 a.m., well before break-fast, exercising Fancy, her yappy, rather anti-social wire-haired fox terrier, on the common in Chesham Bois. It was then a forty-acre sweep of undeveloped land with woods of oak, ash and wild cherry, two ponds, dark hollows and footpaths, all bordered by North Road and South Road. Its outskirts were just a step across the road from the doctor's three-storey, Tudor-style, semi-detached house called Ashlyn in North Road. She'd bought the house, built in 1906, on land owned by Liberty of London, in 1954. And like larger detached properties in this select residential road it occupied a large plot with open views across the common, perfect for feeding Helen's lifelong passion for the countryside. She enjoyed the early morning light where she could watch the sky and see the woodland change from green to gold. As usual she heard the cawing of rooks that colonised the treetops opposite her front door.

Helen left her home around mid-morning, driving her Hillman Minx car to the neighbouring village of Hyde Heath via Copperkins Lane, a distance of about two and a half miles from Chesham Bois, where she would be making a house call to a patient in Meadow Way, the council estate off Brays Lane. Hyde Heath then was a village of medium and large houses and the council estate, and suffered from divided class distinction lines. Everyone knew their place and knew each other but did not necessarily mix.

On her way she would have been noticeable driving her pale blue saloon car along Weedon Hill, the main road through the village linking Chesham and Great Missenden, with Fancy on sentry duty on the seat beside her. Despite the 9 million cars on British roads in 1966 they were still a rarity in the village. Eight cars, six motorcycles, two three-wheelers, and numerous bicycles were about average for the village. Standing well back on the left on a large plot of land, a quarter of a mile from the centre of the village and only vaguely visible from the road, was a small, shabby, 1920s bungalow called Rosemead. It was approached by a rickety wooden gate and long, narrow path. A wooden veranda ran along the front of the property, to the side was an assortment of dilapidated outbuildings, a shed, broken-down greenhouses and an old garage. The overgrown front garden ensured no one was welcome. This was the house in which Dr Davidson had attended Herbert Baker's invalid wife Ruby until her death in 1960, aged 70. When Herbert moved out of Rosemead in September 1961 to live at Ashlyn in Chesham Bois following his sudden marriage to the doctor, he left Rosemead in the hands of his long-standing housekeeper Kathleen Cook until her death. A withdrawn, plain-looking woman who kept herself to herself, and never part of the Hyde Heath community, Kathleen was of small stature, but strong, fit and capable of doing anything physical. What is more, after thirty years in service for the Bakers, and having cared for Ruby over years of her prolonged illness, she had become very attached to Herbert.

The doctor passed Hawthorns, the detached house next door but one to Rosemead, home to local builder Michael Baughan, then almost immediately on the right was Hyde Heath Infant School where two days before the children had returned from half-term holiday. Dennis Silcocks, the school's head teacher from 1964 to 1970, recalled seeing the doctor drive through the village occasionally, which he described as 'a welcome novelty, something to punctuate the day. The usual in the traffic sense was nothing very much, there were few cars.' He remembered conversations with Helen, how he made a point of stopping to chat about their mutual interest in flora on the common next to the school.

Helen and Herbert were regular churchgoers. Every Sunday they attended the tiny St Andrews Church of England church that stood behind the school. The vicar of Little Missenden, the Reverend Francis Roberts, officiated there, and it was where Herbert Baker, a faithful benefactor to the church, had been a lay reader for many years. Helen had a good Christian upbringing, learning as a student at Sherborne School for Girls, the top public school in Dorset at the forefront of women's education, that there was no place for spite, gossip, slander or petty-mindedness. Girls at Sherborne were brought up remembering their forefathers had crossed oceans and mountains in obedience of the teaching of Christ.

Opposite the church Helen turned left into Brays Lane, passing familiar landmarks at the heart of the village: the Post Office and stores on the corner, run for years by the Murrell family, was the centre of everything, from where local gossip spread quickly; the Memorial Hall; the Baptist Chapel; and the cherished red telephone box, a working lifeline in those days when most people didn't have a phone in the home. Even the local policeman, armed with pennies, phoned into the police station from there. Brays Lane was a busy thoroughfare, another world, with a constant stream of people either walking or on bicycles. Almost everyone in the lane kept chickens and all had vegetable plots. She passed the small, white pebble-dashed wool shop where in the summer so many house martins nested in the soffits under the roof that windows could not be opened until the young had flown. The turning into Meadow Way where the Swains family lived in a post-war council house was halfway down on the left. Helen Davidson looked in unannounced that morning to check on the Swains's 2-week-old twin girls. That's the way she was. This doctor had brought a new kind of caring to the community.

As usual on his wife's afternoon off, Herbert Baker, who had a substantial private income, left home at 1.35 p.m. precisely, after a light lunch to go to a part-time clerical job in Chesham. Herbert and Helen would be dining out that evening in Hyde Heath with their friends, the Reverend Francis Roberts and his wife Gwenda, at the vicarage in Chalk Lane. Unusually that afternoon Herbert left his black Morris 10 in the garage. Instead he caught the 353 double-decker bus down the road at Anne's Corner, for the nine-minute journey to Chesham. He would be out till 5.30 p.m. He was over 80 years old, having finally retired in 1954 from Grindley and Co. bank in the City of London, but he liked to keep himself busy.

On Wednesday afternoons when Herbert Baker had left for work Kathleen Cook also had a regular arrangement. She travelled from Rosemead in Hyde Heath to clean and cook for Dr Davidson in Chesham Bois, and to answer the phone. These were the days before answerphones and mobile phones and doctors needed somebody around to take calls when they were out. This was particularly important for Helen who, in addition to her usual duties, was on a list of police doctors and called upon as needed for alleged cases of rape, domestic violence, to assess the mental health of detained persons, and to take blood samples. Sometimes Kathleen cycled to Ashlyn. More often she caught the hourly, single-decker bus which dropped her at the southern end of Copperkins Lane near a large, pebble-dashed detached house called Copperkins, set in a wide gravelled drive. From there she walked to Ashlyn. Against her better judgement, Helen had agreed to Herbert's suggestion that Kathleen should come once a week to clean the house. She refused his original plan to have her at Ashlyn as a housekeeper living on the top floor. After five years of marriage, Helen was uneasy with his fixed ideas; they intruded on her privacy. She didn't tolerate having to obey orders.

After Herbert Baker's departure and Kathleen Cook's arrival at Ashlyn, Helen left home at about 2.30 p.m. and drove to Amersham on the Hill, three quarters of a mile away. It's the new part of Amersham, north of the picturesque old town, colloquially termed Top Amersham, which grew up around the station with the arrival of the Metropolitan Railway in 1892. The railway company built new suburban housing estates with a backdrop of woods and fields, which became known as Metroland where commuters could live within easy distance of the railway. By the 1960s, it had acquired a country town feel about it where people shopped locally on foot at thriving independent shops situated mainly in Hill Avenue, Sycamore Road and Oakfield Corner. The streets were virtually clear of cars; parking meters, traffic wardens and yellow lines didn't exist. There were few car parks – they were just not needed. Women pushed prams full of children and buses were the usual form of transport. The doctor called at the Express Dairy, at 41 Hill Avenue, to buy a bottle of milk. The dairy's shop, in front of the main milk depot in Elm Close, was wedged between the Regency Restaurant at number 43, haunt of the Amersham teddy boys, and Tuts, the sports and fancy goods shop. The Express hadn't been in Amersham long and only managed to become a main supplier of milk by buying up milk rounds from small dairymen in the area. In those days milkmen delivered milk to everyone's doorstep, every day of the week including Sundays, so it was unusual that the doctor needed to call in. But she wanted to make a special purchase of Channel Islands, also known as Gold Top, full-fat milk, and it was the only dairy in Amersham that sold it. Gold Top was considered a luxury and was supplied exclusively to the dairy in Hill Avenue by a local farmer who managed a herd of pedigree Jersey cows.

The next sighting of the doctor that afternoon, just a few minutes after she left the Express Dairy, was by Dr Keith Heywood, a 40-year-old GP in Chesham who had known Helen as an anaesthetist at Chesham Cottage Hospital. That afternoon he was having his car filled with petrol at Fosters garage opposite Dr Challoner's Grammar School, in Top Amersham, not far from Oakfield Corner, when he noticed her driving past in her car, travelling south towards Old Amersham on the B441. He remembers commenting to the lad filling his car, 'That was Dr Davidson who has just driven by.'

Helen's next stop in Top Amersham was 99 Station Road, where she called in to see her mother, Mrs Sybil Davidson. They chatted for nearly an hour. Helen had bought this four-bedroom detached house with a large garden, £500,000 in today's money, for her recently widowed, elderly mother who had moved there from Wimbledon in order to be nearer to her daughter. The house, exactly opposite Parsonage Wood, also known as Rectory Wood, separated Top Amersham from the old town.

Helen drove back up to Hill Avenue and parked outside the *Buckinghamshire Advertiser* offices, a few doors up from the

Express Dairy. The time by now was just before 4 p.m. Outside Kerridges, a smart gift shop at the corner of Sycamore Road and Oakfield Corner, and still referred to as the Old Bucks Library that used to be there, she bumped into Dr David Howell who had just finished surgery for the afternoon at his home on the opposite side of the road. He lived in a large detached house with a swimming pool at Oakfield Corner with his wife, who was known by her second name, Rosemary, and their four children. The house was the practice surgery as well as a home. He worked in partnership with Dr Davidson and two other GPs, Dr Rolt and Dr Philips, all of whom were registered at the medical practice in Gore Hill, on the edge of Old Amersham exactly opposite the bus garage. They shared night calls and weekend work and were all members of the very private Chiltern Medical Society. From humble beginnings in the gymnasium at Stoke Mandeville hospital, following the inauguration of the National Health Service in 1948, the Society was set up by local consultants and GPs to provide some form of postgraduate education, share new work and mix socially away from the prying eyes of patients. As the Society evolved, taking on more of a social focus, Dr Davidson, who had been one of its founder members, was rarely seen at functions by workplace colleagues. When Dr Howell saw Helen that afternoon he told me it was 4 p.m. and starting to get dark.

At gone four Helen finally left Top Amersham, travelling south again in her car, passing her mother's house in Station Road. When she reached the junction she turned right into London Road, past Brazil's famous pie-making factory, then turned left into Gore Hill with her GP surgery on the right, and next door to it Piggot's Orchard council housing estate. The road tapered into a steep, narrow, winding lane as she headed into open farmland along the A355 away from Old Amersham in the direction of the market town of Beaconsfield. It was late afternoon as she drove up to Hodgemoor Wood, where parking was easy and her dog Fancy could be safely let off the lead.

It was common knowledge amongst Dr Davidson's patients that Wednesdays were her afternoons off, when she indulged in her passions of walking alone in the local woodlands and birdwatching. In those days not long after the war, ordinary folk considered it a bit unusual for a lady to go birdwatching alone. Many thought it a bit of a luxury, a very upper-class pastime. For Helen the sight of a bird in flight, a spotted woodpecker, a nuthatch, a tree creeper maybe, would make her trip worthwhile, she would let off the day's worries; birds are great relievers of stress.

Suddenly, as she passed Farmer Jarvis's fields at Bury Farm on the left, where cows were grazing close to the road, her car coughed twice then stalled. It had happened before. Helen was well aware that it was one of the killer features of some Hillman Minx cars – they would cut out when hot, particularly on steep hills. Then like clockwork, the flashback. It only lasted a few moments but was enough for the memories of that awful day to come flooding back – memories of the accident too terrible to talk about even to her husband. He didn't know what was going through her head at times. Only she felt the guilt and sadness that had built up over time. 'Please God, forgive me', her deep voice exploded inside her head as the sound of blood rushed through it. A doctor friend, with whom she'd previously confided, had told her they were called fugues: the reliving of past traumas. He said they'd been brought on by the accident. He'd tried to reassure her that over time they would stop. They hadn't. They'd begun a few years ago after her car crash in Amersham. An image of that scene always came to mind. She knew it wouldn't go. The nightmare of pent-up guilt would conflict forever with her strong religious convictions. She remembered how her friend and fellow churchgoer Brig John Cheney, the Chief Constable of Buckinghamshire, personally made sure that adverse publicity at the time of the accident, which could have meant the end of her career as a doctor and impacted on her sensitive work with the police, was controlled. Although her immediate circle of colleagues kept quiet, she felt trapped. How could she live knowing that in a momentary lapse of concentration she was the cause of terrible injuries? The car spluttered and fired back into action. Helen gripped the steering wheel with her gloved hands. That afternoon she was wearing her brown suede, fur-lined gloves. The lurching forward carried her through the moment. She adjusted her eyes on the road ahead. She was back in control.

As usual she parked her car on the left of the junction with Bottrells Lane, opposite the Magpie pub and in full view of passing traffic. Bottrells Lane was a narrow, winding country lane leading to Chalfont St Giles, in places just single track, and bordered by fields, woodland and the occasional farmhouse and assorted outbuildings. The doctor never parked on the large slabs of concrete foundations about 200 yards up Bottrells Lane that provided useful standing for several cars. From 1946 until the early 1960s a large community of Polish servicemen who had fought with the Allies during the war, and their families, had lived in Nissen huts and prefabricated buildings either side of the lane close to Stockings Farm, which was managed by the Pearce family. By 1966 all that was left of the dwellings, church, shop and social hall, neatly tended flowerbeds and kitchen gardens were concrete slabs.

Extending deep into the woodland to the back of Farmer Pearce's fields on the right-hand side of the lane, the make-shift parking area had become a well-known romantic hotspot for courting couples, sometimes amorous police officers. And when it got dark, and no dog walkers were around, it was a notorious homosexual pick-up spot. It was still against the law for a man to have sex with another man. Homosexuals ran the risk of being arrested if caught indulging in what was then considered an act of gross indecency. They had to keep their secret lives secret.

Helen hadn't told her husband that over the last two years she regularly came to Hodgemoor Wood on her afternoon off instead of walking in woods closer to home. She'd decided that, as their marriage was one of convenience, he didn't need to know.

On an Ordnance Survey map of Buckinghamshire, dated June 1961, I pinpointed Hodgemoor Wood, a horseshoe-shaped area of woodland extending to about 300 acres, about three miles from Amersham. It separated the ancient village of Chalfont St Giles, to the east, from the outskirts of Coleshill village, to the west, where it borders Highfield Grove and Seer Green, to the south. It is one of the largest remaining tracts of semi-natural woodland mainly of beech, oak, sweet chestnut and birch in the Buckinghamshire Chilterns and dates back to the thirteenth century. However, late afternoon in November Hodgemoor is not a great place to be unless you are sure of your surroundings. In the 1960s marked paths did not exist, there were nasty old pits from gravel workings, concrete plat-forms and First World War training trenches for the unwary, not to mention tree roots, brambles and concealed ditches under a carpet of brittle leaves. Most people leave Hodgemoor by 4 p.m. on a November afternoon, as soon as the light begins to fade. Dog walkers tend to leave earlier; they don't want their dogs getting lost. In the 1960s, there were poachers in the area and nobody wanted a dog trapped in a snare. Even though you may know your way in the light, it's easy to find yourself in the wrong place when it's getting dark.

By now it was around 4.20 p.m., just about sunset. It was cold and cloudy; it had barely reached 7°C all day. Helen was five miles from home. She straightened her black-and-white checked, tweed skirt, slung a pair of binoculars round her neck and locked her binoculars case inside the car with her black Gladstone bag. She never went anywhere, even when off duty, without the large bag filled with a medley of objects: a stethoscope, thermometer, a patella hammer, a variety of drugs including morphia, something for indigestion and pain relief, gauze pads, prescription pad, and a little money. Working in a country practice, where some houses were miles from a chemist and most patients didn't have phones, she carried as much as she could in case of emergencies.

She dropped the dog lead in the left-hand pocket of her white Terylene mackintosh and the bunch of car keys in the other side. She stood still for a moment peering into the greyness engulfing the woods – her thoughts far away. Was it still the accident that captured her mind? Or was it the rumours in Amersham society circles? She wasn't deaf to the gossip that Herbert was still seeing Kathleen Cook, their cleaner from Hyde Heath, the ill-educated village woman who started life in the workhouse and lived in a different world. Helen knew exactly what Kathleen Cook wanted: her husband.

The feelings passed. She adjusted the clasp of the silver skating boot brooch on her collar that only members of the exclusive Royal Skating Club wore. She checked her wristwatch. It was now well past 4 p.m. – just light enough to walk, and chilly.

She looked above her. It was quiet except for the sudden sound of wood pigeons flying from the treetops with a clattering of wings. Regardless of the imminent darkness she strode away, avoiding brambles and ruts from wartime manoeuvres, beginning to climb the slope into the dense woodland, with her dog off the lead. Groups of small birds, blue tits and chaffinches mainly, wandering through the woods in search of food quickly dispersed as Fancy scampered through dead leaves on the forest floor, barking loudly. His unruly behaviour instantly rendered the area bird-less. It was quickly growing dim and spooky as it always does at twilight.

She headed further up veering to the right, threading her way through giant beeches until she approached the charcoal burners' huge, circular kilns situated on a disused, wartime sewerage works. Not a soul passed her. She was deep in the heart of the woodland. Some would say it was not the time or place for a woman to be walking alone. Helen though, felt comfortable. She'd had it instilled in her not to feel fear. With her public school background and her love and experience of healthy sporting activities – horse riding, fencing and ice-skating – she had learnt confidence and self-control. This is where she felt safe, in the countryside she loved. The fugue was behind her now. Walking in the dark she saw no danger. But it is fear that can save your life. The doctor halted on the brown forest floor in a small clearing at the foot of a beech tree. For once, her aggressive little dog sat quietly at her ankles. It was nearly a mile back to her car.

Helen Davidson did not return home after her walk. At 2.30 p.m. the next day, her body was found along an overgrown track in dense woodland in Hodgemoor Wood, nearly a mile from where she had parked her Hillman Minx car the previous day. It was tragic that the doctor's life should end in the countryside that she loved so much. The killer had struck her across the head with a length of charred timber. Once on her back on the woodland floor, the attacker ground the doctor's head into the earth with a shod foot, gouging her eyes into their sockets. From the horrible mutilation of her face it was clearly overkill. Multiple injuries of this type indicate that the murderer knew his victim well. Her body showed no evidence of sexual assault or any sign she defended herself. There were no witnesses except for her dog Fancy. The killer had time to walk several hundred yards into dense woodland in Hodgemoor Wood on a weekday afternoon, during employment hours, which could have pointed to someone going home after an early shift at work. The Metropolitan Police were called in, the investigation into the murder being led by Det Ch Supt Jack 'Razor' Williams of the Flying Squad at New Scotland Yard. As the doctor had binoculars round her neck Williams deduced she had spied lovers conducting an illicit affair, was spotted, and one or both of them killed her – the killer making sure she wouldn't see again by gouging out her eyes. She had fallen victim to a madman's moment of insanity.

The police recorded it as a motiveless, random killing and that it was not premeditated. The *Bucks Free Press*, published every Friday, held the front page and ran a brief story about the murder in its 11 November edition. The *Oxford Mail*, Oxford's daily newspaper, also published a report that day. The *Buckinghamshire Advertiser* and *Bucks Examiner* had to wait until the following week to report on the murder of the much-loved doctor.

'Razor' Williams was soon reported to be looking for a 'psychopath'. Brig John Cheney, the recently retired Chief Constable of Buckinghamshire, demanded the reinstatement of capital punishment which had been halted two years before. Nothing in the way of useful evidence was found. Despite a major police enquiry with 2,000 people from Amersham and surrounding villages being questioned, the police made no arrest, the murderer was not found, and the file has remained open. In 1971 the *News of the World* newspaper offered a £100,000 reward for information that would lead to the killer's arrest. On the first, tenth, twentieth and thirtieth anniversaries of the murder, the local press resurrected the story of the unsolved crime. At Thames Valley Police headquarters, nearly fifty years later, the murder is one of many cold cases in police files.

2

My Cold Case Investigation: Old Amersham 2009

In February 2009 I was invited to give a talk in Old Amersham about Ruth Ellis, the last woman to be hanged in Britain. It was here that I first met Maria Marston. In a crowded meeting room above the Old Market Hall in the town, a queue of people waited for me to sign copies of *Ruth Ellis: My Sister's Secret Life*, a book I had co-authored with Ruth Ellis's sister. Maria pushed her way through, quickly asked if she could contact me and left.

In an email a few days later, Maria said my research methods had impressed her. She thought I could solve the mystery of the unsolved murder of her family's much-loved doctor, Helen Davidson, in Hodgemoor Wood in 1966. She asked me to look at the case, which was local to the area in which I now had knowledge, and sketched a general outline of the story. She posted newspaper clippings to me about the murder from November and December editions of the *Buckinghamshire Advertiser*, *Bucks Free Press*, *Buckinghamshire Examiner* and *Buckinghamshire Herald* and articles that appeared around the time of anniversaries of the doctor's death. Included in the bundle was an article in a November 1974 edition of the *News of the World* in which the £100,000 reward was offered for information about the unsolved murder case. Maria emphasised her family's close connection with Dr Davidson and her own personal interest. The following typed statement from her mother Fennis Marston was included in the package. Her story got to me:

After our marriage in September 1965 Bob and I were both keen to start a family. Just a few months later I fell pregnant with the first child. Dr Davidson became my GP when I moved to Amersham. The pregnancy progressed normally, or so I thought. The only occasion when I did become somewhat concerned was when a nurse checked the baby and commented that she couldn't hear a heartbeat. My mum reassured me and as no further medical advice was offered or given at this time I carried on as before. The labour did not progress well. I can remember it was frosty and cold as we had an open fire burning. Both sets of parents were downstairs awaiting news and trying to keep warm. My baby boy was finally delivered at home at 9 a.m. on Saturday 22 October 1966. The midwife had remained with me throughout. Dr Davidson was called by the midwife. I can't recall Dr Davidson saying anything to me at this time but my mum who was downstairs was concerned what was happening. Bob's mum suggested she should find out and as mum made her way upstairs, Dr Davidson was coming down and said, 'The baby's head is enlarged. They will need to go to hospital, there isn't much hope, but please go in and see them.'

Bob at some point was told our baby was very ill and unlikely to survive. The baby was so severely disabled not only suffering from Spina Bifida, but internally the majority of the organs in his body were deformed and in the wrong place. Both Bob and I were traumatised at what had happened. The baby was baptised Neil Robert on 22 October 1966 at Amersham General Hospital maternity ward and died at 1 a.m. on 23 October. He had lived for sixteen hours. He was cremated at Chilterns Crematorium in a tiny white coffin. Bob, my dad and bob's mum attended the service. I was physically and mentally unable to do so … I was visited at home by Dr Davidson who stood by my bedside and wept with me. Following this I went to stay with my parents in Chorleywood for a short period of time. It was whilst I was staying with my parents that Bob told me Dr Davidson had been murdered. He was uncertain whether to tell me or not, particularly at that time, but thought I would find out at some point anyway. I simply couldn't believe it had happened, it was tragic and just about two weeks after the birth of Neil. It was too much to take in.

Maria's email was full of questions. She wanted to know who killed the doctor, why it happened, if it had been planned, if someone had followed her, and if it was someone who knew that Wednesday was the doctor's afternoon off. She hoped that maybe a fresh interpretation of existing evidence would increase the chances of finding the killer. She wrote, 'Throughout life there is the inevitable passing of time and things move on, but somehow the death of Dr Davidson stays with us in our hearts and minds and will do forever.'

What could I really hope to add to the original police investigation other than an open mind? After all, catching a murderer was meant to be the job of the police. I had learnt, though, to grasp any opportunities that came my way. And that was how it began. I knew I had to stick with this story of a tragic episode in Amersham's past – it had come to me – it was meant to be. Armed only with Maria's brief description of the murder and newspaper clippings, and balancing the need to quickly find characters from the 1960s before it was too late, and learning about cold cases now, my first task was to make a list of basic questions. No more free time. I was an unpaid (again) private investigator. In front of me the computer screen filled with questions about unknown people in newspaper stories: Dr Davidson, Herbert Baker, police officers, Jack 'Razor' Williams of the Yard, Brig John Cheney the Chief Constable of Buckinghamshire, forensic pathologist David Bowen; places like New Scotland Yard, Hodgemoor Wood, the Express Dairy, Bottrells Lane, Gore Hill and the Army School of Education; everyday life in Amersham, Hyde Heath, Chalfont St Giles, Chesham and Chesham Bois; the NHS; Dr Rolt, Dr Phillips, Dr Howell, local doctors in general practice; bird watching, the Chiltern Hills, Hillman Minx cars and 1960s cars in general; local newspapers, the *Bucks Advertiser, Bucks Herald, Bucks Free Press* and *Bucks Examiner*; bicycles, buses, Top Amersham and Old Amersham. I found myself changing – swopping between then and now. Something inside me had switched a gear.

I soaked up everything about Amersham, searching for leads online and in public libraries. It was like looking for clues through a magnifying glass. I produced page after page of questions. I realised I knew very little, it wouldn't be easy to find answers, the investigation wouldn't be straight forward and it would take determination and legwork. On 1 May 2009 I set off with nine A4 pages of typed questions to meet Maria Marston in Chesham. In her car we headed south towards

Amersham, firstly trying to find Helen Davidson's house in Chesham Bois. At that stage, we had nothing to go on. We were unsuccessful. We visited Hill Avenue in Top Amersham and the location of the Express Dairy in 1966, identifying it by matching the outline of the roof of a new florist's shop with that shown in *A History of Amersham*. From Top Amersham we drove to Little Missenden. There, in a small graveyard hidden at the end of an alley between two houses in the village, we located the grave where Helen Davidson is buried in the same patch of ground as Herbert Baker's first wife Ruby. 'IN CHERISHED MEMORY OF HELEN BAKER (DOCTOR HELEN DAVIDSON)' read a tiny headstone slotted in front of a large one dedicated to Ruby.

Maria and I returned to Amersham. She had shared her family's story with me along with anything known personally to them about Dr Davidson. But before saying goodbye she said, 'As you know, at no time have I done any research into the case. I would love a book about the murder to be published, as would many people in this area. The ball is very much in your court though as to whether the case is worth pursuing.' From now on I was on my own.

An interview had been arranged that afternoon with Tony Dale, a former detective sergeant with Amersham police in the 1960s, and involved in the Dr Davidson case. I'd barely stepped through the front door when he said, 'You're too late. If you'd come two months ago I had press cuttings and photographs in files upstairs, including photographs of the doctor on the mortuary slab after she'd been cleaned up. The injury was right across her face, her eye was split open. A month ago I shredded the lot.'

I started by asking Dale about files on the case:

In those days Amersham police had an amalgamation with Aylesbury. All major files including unsolved murders would be in the police archives as they called them. They just shut them into this big, old, disused garage on the edge of a bigger maintenance garage as was the custom at the time. In 1985 just before I retired I was asked to sort the files out. It was a mess although all the Dr Davidson evidence was still intact in a tea chest in a kind of Pending Tray. Everything was up there then. I am told a civilian took over the job. Whether he kept the stuff as I would … I would use my head as to which we should keep or not keep. An unsolved murder must be kept. I would hope it's still there.

I asked him if there had been other similar murders in the county:

In those days murder in Buckinghamshire was a rarity. Dr Davidson's was the first for a number of years. We had a crop in the early 1970s, mainly domestic, and all cleared up. The main problem we had in the '60s was burglaries at good class houses on the outskirts of Amersham mainly by villains from London.

Dale then reeled off a catalogue of information from forty-three years ago when he was a young police officer, in no particular order. He had clearly told the story many times before and was in full flow: seventy people, mainly women, were walking their dogs in the wood the day Dr Davidson was murdered; house-to-house enquiries were made in the Amersham, Chalfont St Giles, Coleshill, Hyde Heath and Seer Green areas; police interviewed 2,000 males, pulled in all local known villains, half a dozen sex offenders although there was no indication of sexual offence involved, and four psychiatric cases. Several were given a grilling but all had alibis and could not be connected. There was no reason to take fingerprints from any of them as the police had nothing to check them against; Dr Davidson's practice partners, doctors Rolt, Phillips and Howell, told the police about patients they weren't happy with; the doctor had no enemies; a length of bloodstained charred poplar wood, about two and a half feet long, found near the scene of the crime was thought to be the murder weapon. There were other pieces of timber around, burnt remains of wood clearance after felling of some poplars; the doctor had left her bag in her locked car; Herbert Baker's god-daughter initially identified Dr Davidson's body on the slab; despite a murder-mystery article in the *News of the World* in the 1970s offering a £100,000 reward for information about the unsolved murder of Dr Davidson, the police received no calls; Herbert Baker got back from his part-time job at 5.30 p.m. on 9 November 1966; by all accounts Herbert Baker's cleaning lady, whose name Dale didn't remember, was hoping to win the affection of Herbert Baker and was jealous of Dr Davidson; Det Ch Supt Jack Williams of the Yard, who was in charge of the investigation, said the police could draw a fifteen-mile circumference around the town and find the murderer. Dale said Williams looked the part, spoke the part and by Christmas he was back at the Yard ready for retirement. His departure marked the end of the official investigation into the murder, and the case, unsolved, was left with the local police; a freelance photographer was one of the first at the scene of the crime. He snapped his photographs, had the film in the boot of his car before the police had a chance to stop him and before official police photographers arrived, much to their annoyance. 'Who was the photographer?' I asked. 'I don't know,' he replied.

He changed the subject and continued:

I don't mind saying I took an instant dislike to Herbert Baker, a lot of us did – he was a bit odd, too virtuous by far. Two days after the murder the old boy preached an outrageous sermon of forgiveness at the Remembrance Day service at St Andrews Church in Hyde Heath for the person who murdered his wife. The idea of how he could go out and ask for forgiveness for the murderer! Could you? I couldn't. Baker made a statement to the police. There would have been a lot of detail in it. It would all be in the file. You always start with the person who is closest to the victim. He was thoroughly grilled and ruled out. An odd thing happened the following year. He contacted us. He was going on holiday and wanted the binoculars back as he might want them in Scotland – the binoculars that were round his wife's neck when she was murdered. They were sealed for forensics, which is not what it's like now. I don't know if they were given back to him. The fact he asked is weird.

What Dale said next was interesting:

This is something you won't find, something that is not covered in any of the published stories and I can't say too much about it. A bus driver committed suicide in the early 1970s. I've forgotten his name, he was married, he lived with his wife, and I can't say where except it was in the centre of Chalfont St Giles, and it won't be in the main police file. A doctor, now dead, not from the Gore Hill practice, told the police he'd had a patient who was schizophrenic, bisexual, had a very strong sexual urge and was impotent. The doctor said it was a dangerous combination. He drove a bus out of Amersham bus garage, worked as a gardener for someone in Chalfont St Giles and was getting something off his conscience. The doc said it was like lifting the lid off your conscience. I expect they've got a fancy name for it now. The doc said the bloke was psychopathic, quite aggressive, a very mixed up man. Week by week the doctor was drawing him out. The bus driver was due to see the doctor on this particular Friday. Instead he went out in his car with a gallon of petrol to a place at the end of Bottrells Lane in Chalfont St Giles and blew himself up.

I asked Dale how the police took statements from 2,000 males in the area and let the bus driver slip through the net. He said, 'He wasn't on our radar. The only mental hospital locally was The Stone Lunatic Asylum, near Aylesbury. We went through files for inpatients with mental problems early on in the investigation. There was nothing to indicate the bus driver was of interest.' This is where one of my most crucial trails would start, a trail over fifty years old.

Dale then told me about an unnamed motorcyclist who was involved in a road traffic accident with the doctor round about 1965, not long before the murder:

She was driving up Station Road from the direction of Old Amersham and turned right into First Avenue cutting straight into the path of a young man on a motorbike coming down the hill. He drove into her and she was reported for careless driving. It would have all been put in the Incident Book, the Accident Book, the Occurrence Book at the nick. The press were allowed to come in and read them – that's how it was in those days. The Chief Constable Brigadier Cheney was a friend of the doctor –

they went to the same church at Little Missenden and he became personally involved in the incident. Cheney put it out to a private solicitor to make an impartial decision – the names were changed – to see if there was a realistic chance of prosecution. The solicitor said there was no chance of a prosecution and the case didn't come to anything. To my knowledge this sort of intervention was unusual. It had never happened before. I don't think the motorcyclist was badly injured but he started behaving strangely a year or so later. There was a long-running feud between him and the police about Dr Davidson not being prosecuted. He accused the police of a cover-up.

It was an interesting story. Dale couldn't recall the motorcyclist's name, where he lived or worked at the time of the accident, when it happened or whether it was weekend, winter or summer. I picked up the vibes from his description that he regarded the motorcyclist as a troublemaker. Dale was more specific when it came to details of what happened subsequently:

About fifteen years after the murder, well after the other bloke's suicide in Chalfont St Giles, the motorcyclist made a written complaint to the then Chief Superintendent who didn't know about the case, that Dr Davidson had been given special treatment as she was a friend of the Chief Constable. He was trying to stir it up. I had to write a report about the accident on behalf of the Chief Super. It will all be in the murder file.

'Was it swept under the carpet?' I asked. Dale replied, 'No.' At that time Dale was a young police officer, had his own patch in Little Chalfont, a village south east of Amersham, and would not have been aware of all the happenings at Amersham police station. He said the action of the Chief Constable was totally above board and he was 'just being very fair'.

Were the details of the crash in the files Dale spoke about? Did the police question the motorcyclist or his family about the murder? The newspapers reported the doctor had no enemies. Was there a connection between the doctor's crash and her murder some while later? It was obvious that the motorcyclist who, in Dale's words, was not 'badly injured' did have a long-term grievance against the doctor. I knew the next thing I needed to do was attempt to trace the unnamed motorcyclist. I asked Dale if there might be a personal element to her murder. He said, 'We never went into it, it wasn't necessary. It was clear she'd spied lovers and was murdered for it.' At a basic level, even to an untrained eye, the police had blinkered vision. With the binoculars round her neck, that's the way it may have looked. I wasn't convinced. Everything should have seemed important in a murder investigation, not a stone should have been left unturned.

After the interview Dale proposed a guided tour of Hodgemoor Wood to the spot Dr Davidson's body was found. We parked in the same lay-by on the old road where she parked over fifty years ago, then continued up Bottrells Lane to park in the new car park dedicated to the Polish prisoners of war. We walked through the wood to soak up the atmosphere. Dale said everything in the woodland looked different now. As we passed the charcoal burners' kilns he said, 'Charcoal burning isn't something I know about. The workers got turned inside out about the murder because their site was only 300 yards from the scene of the crime.' I tried to imagine that afternoon in 1966 as we headed to the area where the doctor had been found – evergreen trees to the right; beech trees, bare and spindly to our left. It was some distance from the road and not easy to locate due to the passing of time. Dale believed he had found the correct position. But as we carried on walking he stopped and indicated that he was definite about the second location. It was interesting that it was near a distorted tree with a twisted trunk, which stood out from the rest. A rope hung from one of the high branches. According to Dale you could still see the indentation in the ground from the doctor's head three years after the murder.

Between March and April 2009, I wrote twice to Ms Sara Thornton QPM, the Chief Constable of Thames Valley Police at its headquarters in Kidlington, Oxfordshire. I asked if I could see the murder documentation and if Ms Thornton could tell me what level of investigating activity there had been over the last five years in relation to the murder inquiry of Dr Davidson in 1966, what level of resources had been applied, if modern forensic techniques were being used in the investigation, and the likelihood of them solving the crime. I also stated, 'Clearly the manner in which the murderer stamped the doctor's head into the ground points to a character who was sick and desperately in need of help.' Ms Thornton's response was not encouraging:

I am not at liberty to tell you the level of investigation but would like to emphasise that all unresolved homicides within the Thames Valley Police area remain 'open' and are the subject of review ... In any request of this nature we have to ask 'How will the disclosure of this information assist in the investigation' balanced against any distress that the publication may cause any living relatives or friends of the victim ... Taking this into account I do not believe

that further disclosure would benefit our investigation
and that is why your request for further information has
been declined.

I tried to imagine what police officers in the Major Crime
Review Unit at Thames Valley Police were doing now to solve
this cold case. Were they budging from their idea of an unpremeditated killing? They had a theory in 1966; I wanted facts.
What was their version of events now?

I would have to pick up where the police in 1966 left off and
focus on what I considered were gaps in the investigation. With
scant details about police procedure from Tony Dale and their
role in the 1966 investigation, plus his own observations, fragments of evidence, information about an unnamed bus driver
who committed suicide, and a road traffic accident involving
the doctor in the mid-1960s, and newspaper cuttings, but
without Thames Valley Police archive material to work from,
where would I start my search? I would need to get a broader
context of the times, about what was going on locally, collect
background information. I needed to know more than the
police appeared to in 1966. My story owes a lot to a network of
people I enlisted: all Amersham experts who chronicled events
in the area over many years. They all played a pivotal role in
my quest to find witnesses and suspects from forty-five years
ago. They all hoped I would unravel the Dr Davidson mystery.
Day by day I met more people. Somebody would always know
somebody else who would know something.

Over the next three years I used my intuition to find leads.
I placed announcements for information on family history
websites and in local newspapers, I wrote to local studies
libraries, searched through university archives and telephone
directories. I worked on scenarios, then slept on them knowing

my brain would overload if I wasn't careful. I began to pull together strings of those early days of the investigation.

Dr Helen Davidson was not easy to research. There was no biography of her to work from, other than the basics of her education and medical background in the obituary in the *British Medical Journal* dated 10 December 1966, and in *The Times*. Born in 1917 at St John's Wood in London, Helen Davidson was the daughter of Alan and Sybil Davidson. She received her early education at Putney High School and Sherborne School for Girls in Dorset. She won a scholarship to the London School of Medicine for Women in London, graduating Bachelor of Medicine (MB) Bachelor of Surgery (BS) in 1941. In spite of her busy life as a practitioner with an unblemished reputation she was a founder member of the College of General Practitioners and of the Chiltern Medical Society. She was divisional surgeon to the St John Ambulance Brigade, fellow of the Royal Society of Medicine, fellow of the Royal College of Anaesthetists and an anaesthetist at Chesham Cottage Hospital. Beyond medicine her interests lay in ornithology, the countryside, the Amersham Choral Society and more recently in watercolour painting.

My research into official information on births and marriages produced the following results: I found the birth of an unnamed Davidson female child on 1 October 1917, to a mother whose maiden name was Sandilands. Helen's father, Alan Davidson, who registered the birth misspelt his own name on the birth certificate and had to correct it. On Helen and Herbert's marriage certificate, which would normally give the age of bride and groom, their ages were recorded 'of marriageable age'.

I checked with the various medical organisations. It seemed odd to me that St John Ambulance could find no trace of Dr Helen Davidson in its register or in the obituary section of their publication for the year of her death, or the year after. Enquiries with The Royal Society of Medicine (RSM) drew a similar blank. They said they found 'no reference to Dr Helen Davidson'. The Royal College of General Practitioners said that, although she was a member from 1953 until her murder, they had not been able to locate her files, nor did they have any information about Dr Davidson's practice partners at the Gore Hill surgery, in Amersham. The Royal College of Anaesthetists said they had no record of Dr Davidson being a Fellow of the college. It was as if the doctor's existence had been erased. It was only in yearly entries in the BMA Medical Register after she qualified as a doctor that I found more informative entries with a record of her addresses. At the end of the Second World War, she was listed at 77 Eaton Place in London's Belgravia, a classically elegant, white-stoned eighteenth-century residence in one of London's most opulent streets, where some properties formed a select enclave of offices relating to the war effort and the Foreign Office.

In 1966 Dr Davidson was listed at Ashlyn, North Road, Chesham Bois, her phone number Amersham 1841 and surgery Amersham 11. Her name appeared with her three practice partners in Amersham: Dr Rolt, Dr Phillips and Dr Howell. As soon as I saw the reference to the Chiltern Medical Society, I Googled it; there was just one hit. It was an obituary for one of its founder members and past chairman, Dr William Ogden, written by his daughter. Eventually I managed to trace Dr Ogden's widow Barbara and, on 26 March 2009, I spoke to her on the telephone. Dr Ogden and Dr Helen Davidson were amongst a group of doctors who in 1946 started the society in which local GPs and consultants could share new work.

In between investigating threads of the story I considered my role as the narrator of the story. I believe that every victim dies because of who they are, what they are, where they are at a moment in time. The more you know about the victim, the closer you get to the murderer. If the answer to Helen Davidson's murder wasn't in the present in 1966 – after all the police could not find a motive for the unsolved crime or the killer – it was possible that if I investigated her life I might find a reason for her death. I would have to piece together fragments of a stranger's existence, and get to know this dead woman. Over a period of six years I unravelled family histories, previously untold, and built a picture of people involved in the story and what had become of them. I discovered how in the 1960s the lives of three very different local people became entwined.

I did trace someone closely connected to Herbert Baker and asked for an interview via a third party as I felt they would have some answers that could help my investigation. I was told he refused. He said the death of Herbert's wife had caused him very great distress, which heavily impacted on the remainder of the family; his relations have finally moved on and do not wish to revisit that time. I respected his desire for privacy. However, he has no knowledge of others whose lives may have been touched by the murder of Dr Helen Davidson, and wanted closure, or of a wider story that guaranteed the doctor's murderer would not be found.

Several months after our meeting in Amersham I wrote to Tony Dale to ask who the police's chief suspect was. In reply he wrote, 'It's not a thing I can put on paper. And I do not think it would be wise for you to do either. If you know what's good for you, do not mention names.' Dale's advice concerned me. I have made every effort to paint as accurate a picture as possible based on the information Dale gave me nearly five decades after Dr Davidson's murder. It is my intention to keep his story and my own subsequent investigation into the case alive.

3

A Perfect Place for Murder

When Helen Davidson's husband Herbert Baker arrived home from his part-time job in Chesham on Wednesday 9 November 1966 it was about 5.30 p.m. Helen Davidson had not returned from her walk. Some hours passed before Baker eventually reported his wife's absence to the police. He didn't seem unduly worried despite an arrangement to dine with friends, the Reverend Francis Roberts and his wife, that evening at their home in Chalk Lane in Hyde Heath. Baker may have been reluctant to call the police, but the fact remains they were dining out which was unusual; entertaining then was generally done at the weekend, not on a weeknight. Instead of alerting the police immediately, and after phoning Chesham Cottage Hospital to ask if his wife was there (which was odd if they were supposedly dining out), he decided to organise his own search with next-door neighbours in Chesham Bois, and the Rev Roberts. Perhaps his wife was in the habit of coming in late from her solitary walks and he was used to it. However, Baker was born in 1886 and from an era that believed you kept private family matters, private: an attitude not necessarily shared by many younger people in the 1960s. He was a respectable middle-class man with an old-fashioned outlook. He trusted the police but family honour mattered; he did not want a private domestic problem made public. The fear of embarrassing gossip was an overriding deterrent from calling in the police. Under the circumstances it would have seemed quite normal to him to enlist the help of a friend, someone he could trust, to look for his wife.

Amersham magistrate Pamela Appleby described the Rev Roberts as a man of small stature, large ego, highly educated, intellectual and held in high regard. 'Mrs Roberts though was a lovely lady. She was quiet, charming and banked at Barclays in Amersham so I knew her a bit', she said:

> She always looked poverty stricken and down. He was the opposite, always very well turned out, in particular his vestments. They seemed to be more elaborate than those of most Church of England clergy. I felt he was very conscious of his appearance when 'robed'. With practised movement he would swing his cloak so that it opened like a sail and then settled on his shoulders. Anyone within two yards would have been hit in the face but he managed to show off the lovely red lining. He then walked out pretending not to notice the attention. This sounds rather bitchy but it is my recollection of him.

When Baker's search proved useless he contacted the police and reported his wife was missing. At approximately 2 a.m. the next morning, the police found the locked car parked in the lay-by on the Amersham to Beaconsfield road, near Hodgemoor Wood, and a cursory search was made of the section of woodland nearby, but it was soon abandoned – they couldn't do much in the dark. The proper search would have to wait till first light. Herbert Baker and his friends continued their search with a lamp around the unlit country lanes until 4 a.m. The doctor's car was left in the lay-by between Wednesday night and Thursday morning with no police officers guarding it, or guarding access to the woods. In those days blue-and-white tape wasn't used to protect a crime scene. Anyone could have had access to the car and vital evidence could have been compromised.

It was just after 8 a.m. on Thursday 10 November 1966. There had been an overnight frost and a murky grey fog, that took two hours to clear, hung over the Chiltern Hills in the early morning light. Supt Aubrey Smith, the local divisional uniformed commander covering Amersham, Chesham, Beaconsfield and Gerrards Cross, was in charge of the search party. Fifty police officers, including administrative staff plucked from behind their desks at Amersham police station, and 100 cadet soldiers in uniform, from the Army School of Education at Wilton Park in Beaconsfield, had assembled at Stockings Farm in Bottrells Lane. It was the first time in the Army School's history that their cadets had been deployed in a search of this nature but they responded immediately to the request for help from the police. The Army School's usual role was the training of regular and national service personnel who would then be posted to army units to carry out the education of soldiers. They all set off across the dead-leaf carpet of Hodgemoor Wood, close to the lay-by where the doctor had parked her car the previous afternoon.

John Young was a 19-year-old probationary police officer and had been transferred from Amersham police station to Gerrards Cross that day:

I got a phone call early in the morning to go back to Amersham. I didn't get to Gerrards Cross. I joined the search team as a walker on the end of the line of the army unit. There were half a dozen army guys from Wilton Park to every one police officer. We were put in sections, each line walking so many feet apart, then another line like a pattern sweep. They moved us halfway up the hill on the right hand side of Bottrells Lane. I know from conversations that morning there had been a Polish army camp there and there was lots of talk about charcoal.

At 10 a.m. Mr and Mrs Lloyd King were looking out of the window in their tiny lean-to kitchen at Meadow Cottage. The cottage stood in a field managed by their neighbour, Phil Pearce, at Stockings Farm – its dining room windows looked out over Bottrells Lane. Lloyd and his wife, Joyce, witnessed an alarming scene like something from a black-and-white TV police hunt. Joyce recalled that morning:

A row of men holding sticks, dressed in dark clothes appeared in the murkiness, fanning out as far as we could see. They moved slowly in a line, looking for something with their heads down, across the field. The outlook wasn't wooded and there was a footpath that ran alongside the hedge on the other side of the garden on the Stockings Farm side.

Joyce King was a nursing auxiliary and worked part-time at Chesham Cottage Hospital which had just twenty-one beds: seven female, seven male, five children and two private wards. 'It was a GP-run hospital where Dr Davidson practised as an anaesthetist two days a week,' said Joyce. 'General operations like hernias on Thursdays and gynaecological procedures on Fridays. Dr Davidson would have done an outpatients clinic for people who'd had surgery earlier in the day.' Joyce, her husband Lloyd and their daughter Hilary had lived in the Victorian tied cottage, owned by Buckinghamshire County Council, since 1961 – the year that Lloyd became employed as an estate ranger at the county council. Both Joyce and Lloyd had Thursdays off. 'Lloyd worked all over the county in various woodlands,' said Joyce. 'It was a responsible job but he loved it and loved the countryside. He was brought up on a farm and only ever wanted to work outside. He did manual work, went to college to do a hedge-laying course, did litter picking, and at weekends patrolled public areas in Buckinghamshire.You couldn't have found a nicer person – he was a true country gentleman.'

Unknown to the Lloyds, while they watched the happenings through their kitchen window, police officers were calling on their neighbour Phil Pearce, the tenant farmer who managed Stockings Farm.They explained that Dr Helen Davidson was missing, that her car was parked in the lay-by on the main road and asked Mr Pearce if he had seen any sign of her. The officers then asked if they could set up a temporary base at the farm because it was obvious that the doctor would be somewhere in Hodgemoor Wood. Lloyd King wondered what had happened and decided to go across to ask Phil Pearce about it. No sooner had he stepped outside Meadow Cottage, he encountered one of the search party. Joyce King said, 'Evidently one of these lads, not a policeman, spoke to Lloyd. They said they were looking for somebody who was missing. She was known to walk her dog and go bird watching. My husband replied they needed to look in Hodgemoor Wood across the road as that was where people went to birdwatch.'

Also at about 10 a.m., Mrs Pauline Willes, who lived about a mile away at the Old Rectory in Chalfont St Giles, had already received a phone call about the search for Helen Davidson from her brother-in-law, Dr David Howell, Dr Davidson's practice partner. Mrs Willes told me that morning she was driving along Bottrells Lane in a westerly direction when the police stopped her:

> They asked if I knew Dr Davidson was missing, if I'd seen her and where I was going. I told them the doctor often parked her car in the lay-by on the main Amersham to Beaconsfield road and walked her dog in the woods. I told the police I was going to my father's house in Magpie Lane in Coleshill to pick up my elderly aunt who was staying with him. I was worried about her – she wasn't quite right. Then we would be heading to Watford to spend the day there shopping.

Four hours later, at about 2.20 p.m., 50-year-old Ch Insp Thomas Browne, an administrative officer who worked a regular shift from 9 a.m. to 6 p.m. at Amersham police station and who had very little connection with CID, stopped dead in his tracks in the woods. He was ahead of the row of searchers in the woodland and was with one of the young army cadets. In a tiny clearing about 200 yards from the charcoal burners' kilns he saw something like a white heap on the ground ahead of him. Not equipped with telephones, he blew his chrome whistle loudly. Lying there in the countryside that she had loved so much, and some distance from where she'd parked her car, was the dead body of Helen Davidson. Instinctively Browne touched the body to confirm she was dead. Her right arm was raised above her head as if to protect herself and ward off a blow. Her thick sheepskin gloves were covered with dried blood. The army cadet, not used to a sight like this, immediately ran into the bushes and vomited.

Probationary police officer John Young was one of the first police officers to reach the crime scene. He couldn't remember much about that day but what had stuck in his mind was the doctor's dog:

> I saw the body – there were two or three people fairly close to it. The doctor's dog, a terrier-type, didn't let anyone near it. It was near the doctor but it wasn't attached on a lead. If you walked towards the body it went for you. It was quite intimidating. A peculiar animal, if you stepped towards the doctor it bared its teeth. You could only go so far. I seem to remember a request for a dog handler was made.

Young was badly affected by the horror of the scene and spent the next three weeks recovering from the ordeal.

A police officer contacted Dr Kenneth Argles's practice in Old Amersham asking him to come and formally certify Helen Davidson's death. His surgery, though occupying the first floor of the same building as Dr Davidson's in Gore Hill, was not connected to the Rolt, Phillips and Davidson practice downstairs. Mrs Daphne Browne, the part-time receptionist, explained it was Dr Argles's half day and so he was not available. That afternoon he was out walking his new Alsatian puppy. Instead Dr Redman, from his surgery in Sycamore Road in Top Amersham, went to the scene of the crime where he pronounced the victim dead. He transferred responsibility of Helen Davidson's body to the coroner's officer (a police officer at Amersham police station specially allocated to the case) to arrange its transportation in due course to the mortuary.

On Tuesday 23 October 2012, I wrote copiously in my journal. Since my first meeting with retired police officer Det Sgt Tony Dale, I had tried to piece together his account about an unnamed freelance photographer who had reached the murder scene before the official police photographers. That morning I had a breakthrough in my search:

Today after three years of searching I spoke to Malcolm Wade on the telephone at his home in mainland Europe. He's 79 and had just returned from a business trip to Paris. He spoke to me, in his words, 'journalist to another journalist'. In the 1960s he owned a hairdressing salon called Jean in top Amersham. He also ran Elite Press Services, a freelance journalism agency with a photographic studio which he started in 1962, at Elite House located on the corner of Berkhamstead Road and Francis Street in Chesham. Wade said there were two sides to his business that covered the whole of south Buckinghamshire. 'Three or four of us ran the agency working on freelance assignments for local and national newspapers. We had a separate section to do weddings and employed a lady to develop photographs in our film developing unit.' In the freelancing world of journalism in Buckinghamshire everyone knew Malcolm Wade by the ancient sheepskin jacket that was his signature outfit. He said local folk would herald his arrival with, '"Oh look, the *Bucks Examiner* is here" when I arrived in it.' And when it came to reporting local stories it seems Elite Press Services were almost always first on the scene. Wade was also one of a small team of unpaid temporary police officers known as special constables who helped the police in the Chesham, Amersham and Beaconsfield area when needed. He mainly worked nights from 9 p.m. to 5 a.m. because he worked

for Elite during the day. He told me he was first involved
with the story about the missing doctor on the morning
of 10 November during the daily press briefing between
9 and 10 in the morning at Chesham police station. He said
he filed copy to the BBC but was not involved in the search
for the doctor. For the remainder of the morning Wade
said he was 'probably out on a mission'. Malcolm Wade was
very cordial. Then I asked him who the freelance photographer was that got the photographs of the doctor's dead
body before the official police photographers arrived at
Hodgemoor Wood. He said, 'An elderly man with grey hair
called Smith ... staff photographer for the *Bucks Advertiser*
was probably the one who took the photograph of the dog
next to the doctor's legs. He got the photo of the dog ...
the picture that sold the story.' With fifty years of freelancing
behind him he gave next to nothing away. I asked him how
Mr Smith reached the scene so quickly, suggesting he may
have listened in on to police short-wave radio frequency, a
well-practised but illegal technique among freelancers after
an exclusive news scoop. Wade said, 'Smith would never have
done that.'

The news about the murder spread rapidly. Just minutes
after Dr Davidson's body was discovered the freelance photographer arrived at the scene. Having received a telephone
call from an unnamed source he had grabbed his camera, a
Rolleiflex medium format, swung the leather strap around his
neck, found a handful of rolls of 120 black-and-white film,
a flash gun, stashed the lot in the boot of his car and driven
straight to Hodgemoor Wood. Given that the police photographers had not arrived, he was going to get his pictures. He
saw the woman's left arm beside her body, the other stretched

out above her head. Regardless of the body lying face up, blackened, gouged eyes blindly staring up at him, regardless of the small white dog by his mistress's legs baring its teeth, this was his job.

The camera hung round his neck with a taut strap. He held it firmly at waist level with both hands. He took the scene in quickly and set about shooting. Nobody stopped him. He positioned himself so the light fell from behind him on to the body, well back from the snarling dog, calculating the depth of field for the shot. In the focusing ring he could see the top of her white coat splashed with dried blood, a black-and-white checked skirt, brown shoes, the collar of a blouse and a wristwatch on her left hand. He glanced around between photographs. This was unfamiliar territory to him. Never before had he photographed a person brutally murdered. Instinctively he knew the dog beside the doctor's body told *the* story. He wound on rapidly turning the focusing knob, making exposures in rapid succession. Still nobody stopped him. Images of murder: a bloodbath of sheer hatred. Twelve exposures down. He rewound the film, opened the back of the camera, loaded fresh film, cranked the camera to number one, as though his life depended on it. Some of the more explicit photographs showing the doctor's battered head would be banned from publication, though Smith didn't know it then. The article on the front page of the following week's *Buckinghamshire Advertiser*, was devoted to the Dr Davidson murder, giving details of the crime scene and including cropped versions of the photographs taken by the freelance photographer; a few had slipped through the net.

The police soon had Bottrells Lane sealed off to traffic and were only allowing people through who genuinely needed access to their homes. Det Con John Bailey of the Photography

Department of the Buckinghamshire Constabulary was at home when he received the call to attend the crime scene. He drove first to police headquarters in Aylesbury, where his studio was, picked up the police van, then collected Det Sgt George Gaunt. Bailey said:

> I noted in my official police diary that we left Aylesbury HQ at 3.20 p.m. for the scene of the murder. The drive was uneventful. George Gaunt was not the most talkative of people especially when travelling to a major crime. We didn't rush – there was no need. It was dull and dreary when we parked the van in the lay-by on the main road. We always used a grey Austin van, well known to all policemen then, fitted out with the equipment we needed: canvas, tripod, electronic flash, meters, flash bulbs. We set off on foot in our ordinary clothes and shoes to the scene of crime. It took us about a quarter of an hour to reach it by which time it was getting dark in the woodland. It was just after 4 p.m. Police officers were guarding the periphery to keep people away. The forensic pathologist would want to see the scene un-tampered with. Nobody else is allowed. The detective dealing with the case, and the coroner's officer, would have been there first and ensured no one got near the body.

But standard police procedure for guarding the body had broken down. The freelance photographer was eventually stopped from taking further photographs and chased away, but he would have compromised the scene of the crime. It should have been secured by a cordon of police officers but they weren't alert enough to the situation. And there was no blue-and-white crime-scene tape then to seal off onlookers and prevent trace evidence being transferred from one person to another. The freelancer had already secured his rolls of film in the boot of his car. Later on, under the red safe light in his dark room, Smith looked at the grisly images as they appeared in the developing tray.

Bailey read out loud from his police issue notebook, one of many he had stacked in his office at home. 'Photographed the deceased at 4.10 p.m., and at 6.35 p.m., by which time the dog had been removed by Chief Inspector Napier. The dog was there when I arrived and was removed by Chief Inspector Napier. Photographed the body with paper arrows and tape.'

Police officers had repeatedly tried to remove the doctor's dog from beside her body but couldn't get anywhere near it; each time they approached him Fancy snarled viciously baring his teeth to protect his mistress. Det Ch Insp Alfred Napier of the Metropolitan Police Forensic Science Laboratory in Holborn was the only police officer able to defuse Fancy's aggressive behaviour. He took the animal to Stockings Farm, where he was looked after by the Pearce family. Rosalind Pearce was 18, the only child of Phil Pearce and his wife Hazel, who had farmed there since 1954. Rosalind said, 'The poor dog had been in the woods for nearly twenty-four hours and was in shock. We brought him into the kitchen, fed it and gave it a drink. I remember him sitting there, he didn't stop shaking. It had a collar on – not a lead – it had probably been running loose. At about 6 p.m. the police came and took him away.'

Meanwhile, Bailey and Gaunt were taking photographs at the crime scene. Bailey said:

I'd got used to seeing this sort of thing. It didn't affect me. I never batted an eyelid. It was all matter of fact as if I was photographing a beautiful woman. To me it was just

another job. We never knew any of the circumstances surrounding any of the jobs. We had a complete open mind
and got on with the job. We used electronic flash on my
5 by 4 Micro Precision Press half-plate camera. These were
the days when we photographed fingerprints at full size.
I took photographs of the body again at 6.35 p.m. All the
pictures I took were at the scene or at the mortuary. You
take the photos that the Home Office forensic pathologist
asks you to take. You work with them. He's the boss as far as
anything to do with the body. He didn't arrive for ages. That
can be normal. You have to have patience. If you didn't have
any you wouldn't be doing the job. But there are standard
pictures you take before there's any movement of the body
– it's standard procedure, a record.

Det Sgt Tony Dale had been involved on and off that day in
the search. He also recalled a long, cold period of waiting
around in the woods for the Home Office pathologist and
Det Ch Supt Williams from New Scotland Yard to arrive.

Rosalind Pearce remembered the chaos that afternoon at
Stockings Farm:

I got home from work at 5.30 p.m. and there was a policeman
at the bottom of our lane near the main Amersham to
Beaconsfield road. I was oblivious to what was happening.
They had the whole of the lane blocked off and weren't
letting anybody up there other than people who needed
absolute access. When I reached our house police cars were
in the lane outside with their blue lights flashing, goodness
knows why. Our farmyard was chock-a-block with police
cars – they'd got black Austin A55 police cars everywhere,
vans, black Morris Travellers and police dogs. It made access

to the farm impossible. Soldiers from Wilton Park were departing from the lane in lorries. Police officers were constantly in and out of the house, they weren't politely knocking on the door, they'd sort of taken over the whole place. My mum was producing sandwiches and cups of tea and we'd got a farm to run as well, cattle to be milked and so on. They set up what would have been very antiquated equipment by today's standards. I remember they had a special radio which was permanently switched on [with] which they could contact the police out in the woods.

That evening we had friends to dinner which had been planned and couldn't be cancelled. As I recall everything was chaotic in the house between the large police presence, people coming and going, Mum trying to cook dinner, friends showing up who had been stopped by the police at the bottom of the road and having to get clearance to come up to the farm, the doctor's dog being brought in. The dinner friends must have been coming some distance because if they had been local my mother would have cancelled the arrangement.

My mother wrote in her diary that day:

'November 10 – The police find Dr Davidson's body murdered in Hodgemoor. They take over Phil's office. Mary and Hector Ramsey [farmers from North Buckinghamshire] come for a meal. House filled with police.'

It was all pretty amusing as the murder obviously fitted in with lots of social goings-on. It was always pretty busy at the farm with people coming for meals and being close to the December period we were out a lot.

It was after 7 p.m. by the time the Home Office forensic pathologist and his secretary arrived at Stockings Farm.

Phil Pearce loaned them wellington boots in case the route from the farm to the crime scene was boggy. At 7.20 p.m., they were joined by Dept Supt Bowker and Det Insp Barrett of Buckinghamshire police, and Det Ch Insp Napier who led them to Helen Davidson's body. They trudged unsteadily in single file around the edge of Farmer Pearce's fields opposite Stockings Farm, over a barbed wire fence, then through blankets of autumn leaves in the dense, dark woodland to where the body was lying in undergrowth. Other police officers wearing long coats, tall helmets and wellington boots followed the procession. Unlike today, when forensic teams wear white boiler suits, mask, surgical gloves and plastic overshoes to avoid cross contamination, Dr Bowen was not wearing any protective clothing other than wellingtons and a heavy raincoat.

They reached the scene of the crime at 7.30 p.m., some five hours after the body was found. At that time the pathologist was given details about the finding of the body and any other information that the police had discovered before his arrival. Dr Bowen carried out an initial examination of the body in situ, which by then had been garishly lit by arc lights powered by a generator. He noted rigor mortis was fully established in the limbs, that the victim was wearing a light raincoat, the front collar and sleeves patchily covered with blood stains and both gloves appeared to be heavily bloodstained. The strap of a pair of binoculars was around Helen Davidson's neck, the binoculars themselves were lying between the right side of the head and the shoulder – the eyepiece tucked into the shoulder was heavily bloodstained. Bloodstains extended upwards onto her hair and on to leaves immediately to the right of the body, and some further isolated staining was seen at a distance of three feet from the doctor's head.

Det Ch Supt Williams of New Scotland Yard and his colleague Det Sgt Woods arrived at the crime scene in the dark sometime after 9 p.m. Tony Dale was instantly put off by the superintendent's methods. He said, 'His first job was to dish out beer money because that's how they did it at the Met. I was not impressed.' After Dr Bowen's examination of the body, Williams gave the coroner permission to remove it from the woods on a stretcher and loaded into a private ambulance. Dr Bowen and his secretary collected their vehicle from Stockings Farm and followed the ambulance to Amersham Hospital morgue.

It was generally accepted that a small county police force did not have the experience for a murder investigation. Although Brig John Cheney had retired as Chief Constable of Buckinghamshire police a week before the murder, it was left to him to immediately call in officers from New Scotland Yard to assist detectives at Amersham investigate the case. If called out within forty-eight hours of the crime being committed the Home Office met the costs. To small forces like Buckinghamshire this was important; they were always short of money.

All superintendents at New Scotland Yard worked on a rota basis for call-outs outside London. Details of whoever was on call, including their sergeant, were chalked up on a board at the Yard. So when Williams was called out from Central Office to Amersham it would have just been his turn. Jack 'Razor' Williams, warrant number 12157, whose real name was Ernest John Williams, was 59 years old, had come up through the ranks, had three decades of experience in the Metropolitan Police between 1936–66, had served on the Pickpocket Squad of the Flying Squad, and had been presented with the Queen's Police Medal in the New Year Honours List in 1965. He was always well turned out and never seen out without a hat, a prerequisite of the CID then. A man of few words and rather reserved, you could tell the time by him. At 1 p.m. he would leave the office and walk to the local pub for lunch. On a Wednesday he was joined by all his detective inspectors. That was the day they had to produce their staff diaries showing their previous week's work. Williams would personally check each one. Any queries he marked in red ink and expected an answer. He visited all his stations once a week where he checked the crime book in which all allegations were entered in longhand. If he found something amiss he would check it on his next visit. That was how he'd been taught and that's how he lived.

On his Central Record of Service it stated Williams had received fifty police commendations for larceny and robbery arrests. He had not, however, received one commendation for a murder inquiry but nonetheless he headed the investigation into the murder of Dr Davidson. He was near the end of his police service, due to retire in three months' time and was summoned from New Scotland Yard to the Buckinghamshire countryside. This would be his last major investigation.

4

Forensic Evidence Uncovered

I managed to trace Professor David Bowen through his book, *Body of Evidence*, which I had seen advertised on the Internet and had been published in 2003 by Constable (who also published the book I co-wrote about Ruth Ellis). I was looking forward to meeting this doctor who for forty years was one of London's key forensic pathologists and was now Emeritus Professor of Forensic Medicine at the University of London. Bowen had first worked under the renowned forensic pathologist, Donald Teare, then went on to set up the Department of Forensic Medicine at Charing Cross Hospital Medical School. He said on the telephone he remembered the case of Dr Davidson as if it were yesterday, and would show me his personal copies of documentation including his post-mortem report on her. 'It was the most remarkable, most unusual case I had ever seen', he said. 'In those days, especially out of London, murders were an Agatha Christie type of thing.'

In May 2009 I interviewed Professor Bowen, then aged 85, at his home in Hertfordshire. He said:

Looking back to 1966 it was quite emotional because the Department of Forensics at Charing Cross Hospital was only just developing. In London then there were three senior forensic pathologists, Keith Simpson, Francis Camps, and Donald Teare the chap I had worked for: a really wonderful man, a perfect gentleman unlike some of his colleagues. The three of them were referred to by the police as the Three Musketeers and they shared most of the crime work, suspicious deaths and murders in and around London. They were usually accompanied by their secretaries as they travelled across the metropolis working for the London coroners. At that time coroners required reports to be available the day of the examination of the body.

I left Donald Teare at his encouragement because there was a small post at Charing Cross. They'd had nothing much before. I'd been working for ten years on suspicious deaths and jumped at the opportunity.

I was in the department at Charing Cross Hospital when I got the call. It would have been in the afternoon. I had finished my routine work and returned to my tiny room to do the paperwork. In this case in Buckinghamshire I would not have expected to be called out. It was an area of the Home Counties considered no-man's-land regarding crime. They had so few cases. Normally a bigwig like Teare would have been called but he probably said he'd done enough for the day and wasn't going out all that way especially in the dark. He'd find a dinner to go to. Simpson wouldn't have been called, it wasn't his catchment area.

At approximately 9.15 p.m. on 10 November 1966, the body of Dr Davidson was delivered to the door at the back of Amersham Hospital, then through double doors into the morgue where it was placed on the one and only enamel operating table in the middle of the room. It was a small square room with windows high up at the head end of the table, furthest away from the door, so there could be no onlookers. The fridges for dead bodies were on a patio outside. That evening three bodies were undergoing post-mortems.

Tony Dale said the morgue superintendent at Amersham Hospital was a man called George:

> A lovely old chap who was there till 2 a.m. in the morning if it was an important one. He used to smile whatever the time of day. When a body was taken to the morgue there was a book that had to be filled in and a label was put on the toe. That didn't apply that night as the post-mortem was performed immediately.

Mr Herriott, whose wife Vera was the patient with whom Dr Davidson confided about her marriage, was a boiler engineer at Amersham Hospital and was working nights. He was standing at the morgue door when the body arrived. Mrs Herriott recalled her late husband's words to her the following day when he returned from night shift. 'You'd never guess what,' he said, 'Dr Davidson's been murdered.' He described what he'd seen. When they brought her in she still had the binoculars round her neck. She was wearing her tweeds and had a lovely brooch on her lapel. She hadn't been robbed but said her head was like pulp – somebody had battered her. He said it was a terrific sight. They hadn't covered her over. He went up close and looked at her and said it was terrible.

Det Sgt Tony Dale escorted the forensic patholo-gist, Dr David Bowen, to the body in the morgue. A few minutes later identification of the body was made by

Det Con John Childerley, a young police officer on attachment to Amersham police, and by Herbert Baker's god-daughter who cannot be named. By the time the body was ready for post-mortem it was 9.30 p.m., approximately twenty-nine hours after Helen Davidson's assumed death. Police photographers Det Con John Bailey and Det Sgt George Gaunt arrived at the morgue at 9.40 p.m.

Professor Bowen asked me if I would like to see a copy of his post-mortem report. I said I would. I thought to myself this was exactly what I needed — it had never been seen by the public — nobody except high-ranking police officers had this information. Bowen began his report on Charing Cross Hospital Department of Forensic Medicine headed notepaper: 'Post Mortem Examination of Helen Davidson/Baker, aged 54, Reference Number FBF 73, at Amersham General Hospital Mortuary, on 10.11.66 at 9.45 p.m.' Helen Davidson had actually recently celebrated her 49th birthday. Police photographer, John Bailey, had then read from his police notebook: '9.40 p.m. photographed front and sides of deceased's face (left and right) after the face had been cleaned.' Next Bowen recorded the names of everyone present at the post-mortem:

Dept Supt Williams, Central Office NSY
Det Supt Bowker, head of Buckinghamshire CID
Det Ch Insp Barrett, Bucks
Det Ch Insp Napier, Met Laboratory
Det Insp Lund, Bucks
Det Insp White, Bucks
Det Sgt Woods, NSY
Det Sgt Baker, Bucks, Exhibits Officer
Det Sgt Gaunt — photographer
Det Con Bailey — photographer

Professor Bowen told me there would normally be one or two attending a post-mortem but this one was unusual as:

> there was a very strong CID team – ten people observed – I had never had so many. It was a very crowded mortuary – very rare. It was very unusual to drag all those people out at such an unfortunate time of night. Helen my secretary said they hadn't had any crime there of any importance and it was like bees round a honey pot. It was a big event.

Then followed a list of Helen Davidson's clothing:

> Removed in the following order: a pair of brown suede gloves, fur lined; a wristlet watch; brown shoes; a Terylene raincoat with dog lead in left hand pocket; brown woollen pullover; a patterned lined skirt; a handkerchief in right sleeve; brooch on patterned shirt; white full length slip; pink knickers; white girdle; vest and stockings; white brassiere. There was a ring on her right little finger and a wedding ring on the left ring finger.

Then followed 'External Appearances': '5ft 7in in height, and 9–10 stone in weight. Hypostasis was fixed along the back of the body and the liver temperature was 61°F at 10.25 p.m. There was no sign of the clothing being disarranged. [Full details in Appendix.]' And then came the conclusions:

> This woman was quite healthy. The injuries she had received were confined to the face and comprised one large laceration splitting open the left side of the face, and up to half a dozen smaller wounds, the latter being in keeping with multiple blows from a shod foot.

Cause of Death:
1a. Haemophage
due to b. Fracture of the Skull

The estimated time of death was handwritten in pencil below
'External Appearances': 'Time, 4 p.m.–10 p.m. approximately,
about 6 p.m.' Professor Bowen said to me, 'she hadn't returned
for over twenty-four hours ... I had to take into account circumstantial evidence of the estimated time she disappeared.'
Later at the inquest into Helen Davidson's death, and using
muddled police circumstantial evidence, Bowen estimated the
time of death as 4 p.m.

Amongst Professor Bowen's documentation was a list of
items handed to Det Ch Insp Napier of Metropolitan Police
Forensic Laboratory:

List of Samples taken at the scene, (Hodgemoor Wood) and
post-mortem examination, 10 November 1966.

Scene:
Dog hair control
Rose Hip

Post-mortem Amersham General Hospital
Material from wounds? charcoal
Binoculars
Left glove
Right glove
Raincoat
Left shoe
Right shoe
Sweater

Skirt
Blouse
Handkerchief
Left stocking
Right stocking
Slip
Knickers
Roll on
Vest Bra
2 vaginal swabs
Anal swab
Control head hair
Control blood
Stomach contents
Debris from under sheet

I asked Professor Bowen if Dr Davidson had eaten a recent meal. 'Her stomach was half full of food debris and a little fresh blood was present. She died within three or four hours of taking food I guess.'

Professor Bowen pulled out a folder and spread a pile of ten-by-eight-inch black-and-white photographs on the dining table. These I guessed formed part of the secret documentation held by the Major Crime Review Unit at Thames Valley Police. 'According to the local paper,' I said, 'Dr Davidson put up little struggle when she was attacked.'

'There was no struggle at all.'

I asked him to explain that.

'There would be defence injuries on the hands, gripping marks, and there was no debris under her fingernails. Her fingernails were smooth and undamaged.'

It was not surprising that her fingernails were undamaged, I thought to myself. According to his post-mortem report Helen Davidson was wearing heavy sheepskin gloves. Her hands were hardly likely to show signs of self-defence. However, Dr Bowen had also noted in another section of his report that 'both gloves were heavily bloodstained'. This could have signified that Helen Davidson did struggle with her assailant. Professor Bowen continued: 'And the adjacent leaves etc. would have been disturbed in a big way. There would have been signs of a struggle, a kerfuffle. But it was all smooth and tidy. She must have been hit very suddenly. Surrounding shrubs and trees were splattered with blood.'

I was beginning to see clues, the significance of which a pathologist, whose role was medical detection, may have overlooked but which should have been noticed by the investigating team. I realised there could be more to the doctor's death than Dr Bowen's post-mortem revealed. Bowen recalled, 'There were charcoal burners there and she was hit with a piece of wood. It was a piece of wood from the charcoal burners.'

I asked if he knew what type of wood it was.

'No.'

In Professor Bowen's book, *Body of Evidence*, there is a section about unsolved murders in which he refers to Dr Davidson's murder. He states, 'A large piece of burnt wood found at the scene of the crime gave a positive test for blood on its surface, and was almost certainly the murder weapon. The woods had been the subject of tree thinning, and presumably some of the waste wood had been burnt; the bloodstained wood probably came from an old bonfire.' He showed me a letter dated 16 November 1966, from Det Ch Insp Napier of the Metropolitan Police Laboratory in which Napier had

listed exhibits taken possession of at the scene of the crime.
Paragraph two stated:

> Incidentally the large piece of burnt wood found at the
> scene gives a strong reaction for blood, and examination is
> being made to try and identify the pieces of charcoal found
> in the wound with this piece of wood. Perhaps you would
> like to see it sometime? If you would like to telephone me
> I will make the arrangements for you.

What was there to know about Det Ch Insp Napier? In his
'Central Record of Service' there is not much. Alfred Henry
Walter Napier was 46 years old in 1966. He had been in the
police force since he was 26 and was promoted to the rank of
Det Ch Insp when he moved to the Forensic Science Laboratory
in March 1965. He was there just two years. He had received
three police commendations: one in 1950 for his involvement in
a case of robbery; one in 1953 for assistance in a case of murder;
one in 1955 for averting a gang of housebreakers.

For reasons of his own Professor Bowen said he did not reply
to Napier's letter and he did not make contact with the laboratory. There was no DNA fingerprinting then but I could not
understand why he did not follow up on this vital evidence.
I asked him about DNA evidence and if it had been available
in 1966 would they have been able to solve the crime?

'I don't know much about the finer aspects of DNA. I mean,
what specimens could be taken from her? Obviously blood
from the piece of wood. They could have taken specimens but
where do they go from there.'

I thought to myself, there would also have been blood over
the killer, on his hands and down the front of his clothing.
I asked what possessions she had on her.

'She had binoculars, thick suede gloves.' He showed me documents and photographs.

I asked about the doctor's bag that had been found in her locked car.

'I don't remember anything like that.'

A complete list of the doctor's clothing and possessions had been itemised by the Forensic Laboratory. What happened to the doctor's wristwatch? In his notes following his preliminary examination of the body at the scene of the crime, Dr Bowen listed a bracelet wristwatch belonging to Helen Davidson. Police photographer, Det Con John Bailey, was not asked to photograph it. It did not appear on the list of exhibits taken possession of that night by the Metropolitan Police Forensic Laboratory. Dr Davidson's fall to the ground could have been enough to break the balance spring and stop the watch, establishing the exact time of death. The watch disappeared into thin air. Also missing from the items on the Met Laboratory list were the dog lead, a ring from the doctor's right finger and her wedding ring.

Something else caught my attention. The doctor's car was locked when it was found. She left her bag in the locked car. The dog's lead was in her pocket. But her keys were not listed amongst her possessions at the scene of the crime or at the post–mortem. The car keys were not on the body, in the surrounding area or in the car. They were vital evidence. If they weren't on the doctor's person where were they? Their absence surely should have been noted. I asked Professor Bowen if he knew that a freelance press photographer reached the scene of the crime before the police photographers arrived, which didn't go down well with the police, and could have compromised the crime scene. 'That rings a bell', he said.

I asked Professor Bowen if psychological profiles of the kind of person that may have committed the murder, which were carried out in the US in the 1960s, might have helped in this case.

'They would have had to profile almost the whole population.' I mentioned to him that the police interviewed 2,000 people.

'They did try hard,' he said. 'They were a very good team. Nobody could have done better.'

Following the post-mortem, Dr Davidson's body was placed in an oak coffin by Wright Funeral Directors of Great Missenden, who had received a telephone call earlier in the evening from the police requiring their services at Amersham Hospital. They removed the coffin from the mortuary, placed it in their van and took it to the Chapel of Rest in Great Missenden. Dr Bowen and his secretary returned to London. At 11.45 p.m. Det Sgt Gaunt and Det Con Bailey returned to their studio at Aylesbury police headquarters to process their film. John Bailey remembered:

I had to develop and print the films. Nobody helped me. You give evidence to the fact that you're the one that developed the film and haven't retouched the negatives and so on. We were a very efficient, specialised department and we just got on with our work. We didn't have any dealings with anybody but the officer in the case and the forensic pathologist. I went off duty at 1 a.m.

5

The First Forty-eight Hours

The 400-year-old farmhouse at Stockings Farm was now a round-the-clock temporary operations room of a murder inquiry. Det Ch Supt Jack Williams had taken over Phil Pearce's small front office the night before to direct the investigation. It was a small, square-shaped room and its door opened on to the hallway at the bottom of the stairs, which allowed the police to come and go through the front door without unduly affecting the Pearce family. The old oak dining table was covered with files, piles of documents, crumpled balls of paper and handwritten statements on flimsy tissue paper. There was just enough space for two wooden dining chairs. After the first twenty-four hours just one policeman, who was in touch with police in the woods by way of ancient wireless equipment, was posted there.

Phil Pearce's daughter, Rosalind, whose bedroom was directly above the operations room, remembers the police activity at her home:

I remember going in the office one evening to take the policeman a drink and the radio walkie-talkie was switched on. Suddenly there was a loud noise and I said, 'What's that?' He said, 'One of our lads just fell out of his tree' which I found vastly amusing. But absolutely nothing changed about life on the farm with the murder. You have to understand that farmers and their families tend to be pretty down to earth people and used to seeing and dealing with death. Granted, not human murders, but it wasn't something that caused loads of upheaval in our lives other than the police presence and obviously wondering who the murderer was. My mother wrote in her diary that day, 'Police move into Phil's office first thing in the morning. All forces searching for clues'. I do remember the police kept coming in and out talking to my father, and I was told not to stop my car late at night if anyone stepped out of the woods and flagged me down. Also my father told me if I got a puncture on Bottrells Lane to just keep driving on it. I think I did make more effort to lock the back door when my parents were out late at night when I was on my own. For several years we had no lock on the front door and just a hedging stake with a large sack of wheat propped up against it keeping the door shut. The murder changed everything. It made us more security conscious.

On Friday morning at the request of Det Ch Supt Jack Williams, police photographer Det Con John Bailey drove once more from Aylesbury to Hodgemoor Wood where he took photographs at the crime scene. Reading from his police issue notebook, 'I returned at 11.30 a.m. with Chief Inspector Napier, photographed dent in ground where body was found. Photographed small sapling and hole with a ruler. At 12 p.m.

went to Amersham police station. 2 p.m. returned to studio in Aylesbury. 6 p.m. off duty.'

This was a murder investigation but Williams had not asked Det Sgt Gaunt or Det Con Bailey to photograph the windows, side mirrors or bodywork of Dr Davidson's car for fingerprints. The car was not even examined. It seems Williams felt there was no reason to search it and little attempt was made to preserve the parked vehicle from contamination or protect any evidence. Having made assumptions based on the binoculars around the doctor's neck and having already decided she was the victim of a random attack and not pre-meditated, within twenty-four hours of the body being found, Williams permitted Herbert Baker to drive his wife's car away from the crime scene. Baker drove it back down to Amersham to the bottom of Gore Hill, then into the medical practice's car park on the left. He parked it in Helen Davidson's usual space on the gravel drive, on the left-hand side of the surgery facing the privet hedge. Mrs Daphne Browne, wife of Ch Insp Thomas Browne who found Dr Davidson's body, was a part-time receptionist and medical secretary for Dr Argles and his practice partner Dr Kay on the first floor of the Gore Hill medical centre. Mrs Browne told me she remembered seeing the Hillman Minx in the car park:

> It was quite weird that Mr Baker should drive the car to the surgery car park and leave it there. It was thoughtless if nothing else. I went downstairs to talk to the receptionists in the surgery that morning and they asked me if I'd seen it. It really upset all the staff there.

Det Ch Supt Jack Williams was only looking in one direction. From the very beginning of the murder investigation he was dogmatically sticking with the lovers theory: through her binoculars Dr Davidson had seen lovers who shouldn't have been there; the murder had been impulsive; it was carried out in a moment of unpremeditated madness; and it was motiveless. His opinion was that the murder was carried out by a 'nutter' and it was as simple as that. Williams was reported in local newspapers as saying 'the binoculars round her neck caused her death'. Was it that simple though? It was almost as if there was nothing more to investigate.

As the senior murder investigating officer, Williams would have known that the first forty-eight hours in any investigation are the most important and if an arrest is not made within that time the chances of solving the case rapidly decrease. The reason is that each passing hour gives the suspect more time to flee and crucial evidence more time to be lost. But instead of being open-minded, Williams immediately boxed himself in, making assumptions, and seemed wilfully blind to any other theory. He did not consider it could have been a planned murder by someone the doctor knew. Did he not consider that the doctor may have seen lovers who had connections with her? What if the killer were a psychiatric case that the doctors in the Amersham area weren't aware of, someone who'd managed to keep their problem out of sight? Whoever murdered the doctor and mutilated her face and eyes must have been horribly disturbed, had strong feelings, somehow remained undiscovered and must have normally shown great self-control. Someone who had a respectable job? What if it was overkill because the murderer knew the doctor and what she represented: her connection with hospitals, how she was highly regarded in society and had a lot to lose? Was it this that triggered a reaction in the killer because she had known them?

In spite of newspaper headlines, 'Illicit Lovers May Have Killed Doctor, Says CID' and 'Murder of Woman Doctor "Motiveless"', in private some senior police officers were convinced it was not a random murder. Mrs Hazel Pearce from Stockings Farm had expressed her concern to the police that her daughter Rosalind still kept going back into the woods alone, riding her horse and walking the dogs. Rosalind told me:

> A police officer told my parents very early on in the investigation that this wasn't a random murder, that they were convinced the killer was someone who knew Dr Davidson, so they weren't dealing with a serial killer, and there was no need to worry. The information had obviously come from the pathologist that she knew her attacker, because there were no defensive blows upon her body. I do know that the police were pretty certain that she knew her attacker. They said that in their opinion this was a one-off murder because they knew one another. I remember so clearly, and not being told it once, but on a number of occasions. At that time my father knew one of the commanders who had said they pretty much knew who the killer was but that the person had a cast-iron alibi that they couldn't break. They didn't have the evidence. They said that if they put a rope round our farm, within a radius of fifteen miles, the person lives within it.

Two more of my interviewees shared the opinion that it was not a random murder. Dr David Howell who had been Dr Davidson's practice partner told me, 'It was thought to be a specific thing. I knew one of the police well – he intimated they knew who'd done it.' During my interview with forensic pathologist Professor Bowen I asked if it was possible Helen Davidson knew her killer. 'Oh yes,' he said:

> and the simplest and most naive explanation is that she was in the wood with her binoculars, saw one or two people who shouldn't have been there. But there was a specific reason why she was brutally murdered. Now then, what happened there? I think she had seen something that was very important to somebody and which on no account should be seen. Now at that time, who else would be in the wood? I think they were local lovers. The person must have recognised her immediately although she was well wrapped up. It couldn't have been the old boy, her husband.

Shortly before his death in 2011, Professor Bowen confirmed in a letter to me that as the injuries to Dr Davidson's head were confined to the left side of her face, it would appear that 'the killer was not standing behind her during the attack'. In other words, killer and victim faced each other.

In any case of murder the police should have wanted to know as much as possible about the victim and, especially in this case, Helen Davidson's normal pattern of behaviour. Gaining an understanding of why a victim was selected at a particular place or time could have led police to the criminal. Tony Dale said the police had not looked into Helen Davidson's background – they weren't interested. I needed to find out as much as I could about her because the clearer the picture I had, and the more I knew her, the more chance there would be of finding clues as to who killed her. I was beginning to wonder if the police were not budging from their blinkered opinions for fear of confronting awkward situations and finding something disagreeable about the doctor. I needed to know Helen Davidson more than the police appeared to in 1966.

What made the killer go out suddenly and commit a one-off crime? There would probably have been some sort of emotional build up. Dr David Howell said, 'My wife and I thought it would have been a psychiatric chap. It was so bizarre that her eyes were gouged out.' The more I thought about it the more things did not add up. Dr Davidson may have seen lovers, but an affair between a man and woman is not in itself a criminal act, and to murder for it seemed like overkill. This had more deliberate elements than just some random killing. The grinding of the doctor's eyes bore the killer's unique style.

Policing was less sophisticated then compared to what it is now. Techniques for solving crimes have much improved. Criminal behaviour profiling nowadays can probably tell you what the murderer was like, why he committed the crime. Today the police have more sophisticated methods of finding their 'man' than they did in 1966. In the US in the 1960s psychological profiles of the kind of person who might be driven to kill like this (grinding the face into the ground) were put together. Creating a psychological profile of the killer – could this have helped the police?

The police's belief that there was no sexual motive because the doctor had not been sexually assaulted, I found unconvincing. It was no reason to assume that sex was not involved in the murder. It did not occur to them that someone with strong sexual feelings might be impotent, homosexual, or both. The killer could have felt persecuted for being homosexual, which was part of his complex problems, lacking in self-esteem with deep-seated feelings of inadequacy. A paranoid schizophrenic holding at bay a troubled mind, and who had a secret life as a homosexual, could be lethal. Who was the killer with that

afternoon? Was it somebody the doctor knew? Could the
doctor, armed with this information of a secret liaison, destroy
his life? Det Sgt Tony Dale said they questioned 'all those with
convictions or suspicion of sexual offences, although there was
no indication of sexual offence involved. We were aware that
peeping toms or flashers could be suspect. Several were given a
grilling but all had alibis and could not be connected.'

It was only the *Buckinghamshire Examiner* in their
2 December 1966 edition that published an addition to the
police's 'courting couple' theory. It stated that on the Monday of
that week Det Ch Supt Williams, at a surprise press conference,
took the unprecedented step of asking the public if anyone
knew of any 'illicit love affairs' in Amersham. He admitted it was
a unique step, but that it was an unusual murder. Then he hinted
about homosexual liaisons saying, 'police had not ruled out the
idea that Dr Davidson may have disturbed two homosexuals in
the wood'. Two thousand men were apparently questioned but
had the police sent anyone undercover to investigate the secret
world of homosexuality in the area?

During a press conference at Amersham police station
Williams appealed for information about 'illicit love affairs'.
He said the murderer may have thought the woman with the
binoculars was an inquiry agent, 'watching to help divorce
proceedings. The couple could have been a well-to-do businessman and his secretary. Whoever it was, it would appear
that they tried to put her eyes out of action and then stamped
on the binoculars making sure she would never see anything
again.' I found the police explanation unconvincing. It was
only one interpretation of a motive for murder and I wasn't
going to let police theories colour my judgement.

The peculiar grinding of the doctor's eyes into her skull,
mutilating her face, rendering her unrecognisable, bore the

killer's signature. It suggested an attack on the doctor's character, an outpouring of sheer hatred. It was clearly overkill, her identity being the target of the attack. There was frenzy in the attack, which indicated the work of a fanatic. To me, multiple injuries of this type suggested it was specific, someone who knew their victim personally and hated her. This was an obvious profile of a man with a grudge, maybe against women, because of his own deep-seated inadequacies. Once the doctor was on her back on the earth the attacker had time to grind her eyes into her skull and then into the earth with a shod foot before making his exit from the scene. He was not in a hurry, was probably confident the body would lie undiscovered for many hours and had time to make his escape and dispose of any clothes that were bloodied in the attack. It suggests he knew his surroundings well, lived in the area and had an accomplice to help him dispose of bloodstained garments.

The crime scene was tidy as if the murderer had taken great care not to incriminate himself. There was no trail of footprints in the dried leaves. Yet he left a length of bloodstained burnt wood, supposedly the murder weapon, fairly close to the scene of the crime. Why leave behind such an obvious clue? Why would a murderer who presumably wants to avoid detection leave the weapon so close to the scene? Was the person sane? If not, how did he slip through the net? This, it appeared, was hatred.

Professor Bowen may have thought there was no sign of a struggle, that the 'doctor's hands and nails were clean, she hadn't tried to protect herself' and the scene of the crime was not in disarray. Was it correct to assume though that Helen Davidson hadn't tried to defend herself before she fell to the ground? According to Bowen's own post-mortem report the thick sheepskin gloves that she was wearing were thick with dried blood. This could have signified she put out her arms in self-defence. The murder scene was left neat and tidy: another signature of the killer. The length of wood would have taken some strength to wield. If there was blood on the length of wood there would have been blood on the killer, on his hands and down the front of his clothing. How did the murderer get away from the murder scene, splattered with blood, without someone seeing him? He would have needed an accomplice to help dispose of or wash his garments. Someone he could trust: a wife?

Lloyd King and his 14-year-old daughter Hilary from Meadow Cottage, and Phil Pearce and his daughter Rosalind from Stockings Farm, ventured into Hodgemoor Wood specifically to look at the place where the doctor was murdered. Rosalind's mother wrote in her diary for Saturday 12 November 1966: 'Hilary [King] comes over this morning. Phil, Lloyd and the girls go over to murder spot.' Rosalind Pearce said: 'All I remember, because I was such a gory kid, was asking my father to take me to the place where the body was found. Whether he [Phil Pearce] was with them when they found the body, or accompanied the pathologist to the spot, I can't be certain but he knew exactly where it was. I wasn't scared. I was more excited about the whole thing.' Hilary King described the crime scene as well, located off the beaten track:

We went past the charcoal burners' kilns then into a bit of woodland where we didn't go to usually. What impressed me about the scene of crime was that it wasn't the usual spot where people walked. They either went to the top half of Hodgemoor Wood [closer to Chalfont St Giles] or the bottom half [by the makeshift lay-by in Bottrells lane]. This was in the middle. The impression I had going there, golly, this is a different place to where people would have gone. It's not a place we knew. You could still see the remains of the sticky blood and the deep hole in the ground made by the doctor's head.

Rosalind Pearce described how she looked with fascination at the blood spattered across the trees:

There was almost a clearing but not much bigger than twelve feet in diameter, her body had been in the middle. We made comment at the time about the fact of how wide the red blood spatter was, roughly at shoulder height around the trees and undergrowth, and that the murderer must have been covered in blood. One thing I am very clear on is that there were absolutely no police at the scene.

Information about the blood spattering on the trees was confirmed in Dr David Bowen's secret post-mortem report but not mentioned in the press. Had the police suppressed this evidence?

Another factor, which for some reason had not been reported in the newspapers, and obvious by its absence, was that Dr Davidson was a lady of habit. Many patients and other people knew she had Wednesday afternoons off when she made regular birdwatching visits to the woods with her dog. Maybe the police did not consider it important. It almost seems they were so fixed on their theory of the random killing that they had ignored a huge clue in their murder investigation: that the killer may have known the doctor's movements.

Razor Williams's request for help about Dr Davidson's dog, at a press conference held at Amersham police station, and reported in the *Bucks Free Press*, was confusing. Williams thought that Dr Davidson's wire-haired fox terrier, known to be unreliable to strangers, may have bitten his mistress's killer. He asked for information about anyone having been bitten by a dog on the hand or leg. 'We have checked with doctors and hospitals,' proclaimed Williams, 'but it is probable that if the dog did bite the killer, he treated it himself or perhaps went to the chemist. But a dog bite could be difficult to hide and someone may have noticed at a time that would coincide with the murder.' Once again were the police looking at the scenario the wrong way? Had it not occurred to them that the opposite or alternative situation was equally important? Was it invisible to them that Dr Davidson and her dog may have been well known to her attacker, and a possible accomplice, who knew the dog and with whom the dog felt comfortable? It is unlikely one person could have attacked and killed the doctor alone. While he took his time stamping on the doctor's head, grinding it into the ground, there had to be someone else there to keep the dog away. I guessed it had to be someone who knew Fancy and felt comfortable with him. The killer must have had an accomplice and was known to the doctor.

The killer had walked some distance into the woods on a Wednesday afternoon, an odd time to commit murder. Didn't he have a job? It was an era of almost full employment in the UK. Was it someone who finished work early? Could it have been a shift worker on his way home? Also noticeable by its absence in the newspapers was any mention of the lovers' makeshift car parks in Bottrells Lane. I considered statements given to me by people who lived and worked close by: Rosalind Pearce and Joyce and Hilary King, and

Mr David Mulkern, one of the charcoal burners who worked in Hodgemoor Wood in 1966 whom I'd traced early on in my investigation. It was common knowledge that lovers stayed inside their cars on the concrete lay-bys, which extended deep into the woodland. Rosalind Pearce said:

> It was rare for the car parks to be empty. Cars were in and out during the day. It was funny, about lunchtime and at about 4.30 in the afternoon you'd see a man driving his car in and shortly after another person would drive in. I used to ride my horse and walk in the woods. The next thing you'd see was one of the cars very steamed up. There was a lot of that. We had cattle and sheep in the fields and I remember one of my father's cows jumped over the barbed wire fence and landed on top of the bonnet of a car parked there. The man tried to sue my father.

Nor was it likely that lovers would have ventured near the overgrown spot where the doctor's body was found. Mr Mulkern, the charcoal burner who depended on the woods for his livelihood and whose kilns were 300 yards away from the spot where Dr Davidson was killed, said:

> Absolute rubbish. She was nowhere near where they [lovers] used to go courting. They parked on the concrete lay-bys but didn't go into the woods. Nobody would have chosen that place where she was found. I used to go back at night sometimes, and hang around till one or two in the morning, watching the kilns if they weren't cooked and it wasn't pleasant going there in the dark. It was a strange sort of place at that time. I wouldn't have chosen that place almost in sight of our yard. If couples had come in our direction

they'd be seen, stood a chance of being observed by us or by anyone working in the field. The courting couple thing was rubbish.

What *was* the killer doing in the woods in the dark?

6

The Wealthy Davidsons

Early in my investigation I found factual errors in press reports about Helen Davidson and her husband Herbert Baker. Some said there was a twenty-year age difference when it was actually thirty years. Most publications reported her age incorrectly as 54 at the time of her murder when she was in fact 49. Dr David Bowen's post-mortem report also recorded her age as 54. I wondered about the police work, their form filling, about information given to them by Helen's next-of-kin, her husband Herbert Baker, and the role of the police in supplying official data. They clearly hadn't checked all the details. And it was generally reported in the newspapers that Helen Davidson was born in Scotland when she was actually born in London. Most reported only snippets of personal information: how long she had been practising as a GP in Amersham; how she had been married to Herbert Baker for five years; how she continued using her maiden name. Nothing was known about her early life other than she attended Sherborne School for Girls. Only twice did the newspapers make passing reference to members of Helen's family. Firstly in the 24 November 1966 edition of the *Buckinghamshire Advertiser*, Helen's brother Anthony expressed his thanks 'on behalf of the doctor's relatives ... for setting up the Helen Davidson Memorial Fund ... and to everyone who has shown such kindness and sympathy to them'. Secondly the *Bucks Free Press* mentioned a house Helen Davidson bought in Amersham for her unnamed 82-year-old mother.

Apart from these brief references, the doctor's family kept their private affairs private. I couldn't just leave it. I had to explore all avenues. My instincts told me that her murder fifty years ago was more complicated than a spur of the moment affair. If top police officers could not solve the murder I wondered if clues could lie in the doctor's background about which virtually nothing was known. I believe Helen died because of who she was, what she did, her background. Anything that happened in the last few weeks of Helen Davidson's life, or which began long before 9 November 1966, could be important. Present events are often rooted in the past. I needed to reconstruct the forty-nine years of Helen Davidson's life, build up a picture – the real facts about her, and her circle – dig deep into her past and gain a feeling about her relationships. Without that I had little chance of making any progress in the investigation or discovering a motive for the murder. Family history could be relevant.

I delved into Helen's life, checking on where she came from, travelling to places she visited, looking for clues amongst census records, birth, death, marriage and electoral registers and researching previously unseen academic records. I found that in 1912 Helen's father Alan Davidson married 30-year-old Sybil Emily Sandilands. Very little is known about Sybil other than she was the daughter of Alice (née Faber) and Edwin

Charles Sandilands who was named in *Burke's Landed Gentry of Great Britain*. The birth of Alan and Sybil's only daughter, Helen, at home in Hamilton Terrace, St John's Wood, London, on 1 October 1917, was registered the same day by Alan Davidson. He had misspelt his first name on the birth certificate then had to correct it. No first name is recorded for his daughter, just 'girl', which was unusual but not unknown. His occupation was given as company secretary.

In the early 1920s, Alan Davidson and his family moved from St John's Wood to 'Sandys', a substantial house in Portinscale Road, a wide tree-lined road in Putney, South West London. They lived next door but one to the influential Attlee family whose son Clement became Leader of the Labour Party in 1935, deputy prime minister for most of the Second World War and subsequently prime minister for six years in 1945–51.

Helen Davidson was a girl born into the upper-middle class, had a privileged upbringing and was certainly marked out from birth to achieve greatness. There was more to this lady than newspaper articles about her murder would suggest. As a young girl she attended the Convent of the Sacred Heart School, which was close to the family home. Then, at the independently run Putney High School for Girls, where she was a pupil from 1926–30, Helen developed her love for the countryside. Aged only 11, there was an awareness and sensitivity for country folk expressed in her piece of prose that was published in the literary section of the 1928–29 school magazine. Her atmospheric essay about a gypsy family travelling through country lanes also gave an indication of the passion she developed for the countryside in her later life. During this time, according to Putney High School handwritten record books, Alan Davidson was 'company secretary for a paper manufacturer'.

In 1930 the national school leaving age was 14, and only those whose family could afford to send their children to grammar school had any hope of secondary education. In September 1930, Helen Davidson aged nearly 13 became a boarder at Sherborne School for Girls, the top public school in Dorset at the forefront of women's education for girls with wealthy parents. The school was established in 1899, in forty acres, on the edge of the market town of Sherborne overlooking countryside. Helen was in Thurston House, named after the 11th Abbot of Sherborne. In 1930 Miss Hilda Stuart became headmistress. Her eccentric brilliance, her formidable mind, fresh ideas and devotion to the school had an enormous impact on the girls. Her appearance was legendary. Year in year out, she wore a shapeless Harris Tweed coat and skirt over which her black gown ballooned out as she strode through the school like a galleon in full sale. She was a great orator, she brushed aside class snobbery, and she had visions of all her girls in careers.

The school was founded on the Evangelical denomination of the Church of England. Girls were brought up remembering their forefathers had crossed oceans and mountains in obedience to the teaching of Christ and were taught tolerance, kindness and self-reliance. On Sundays at 8 a.m., while maids slopped out the girls' china washbasins, the students dressed in long-sleeved dresses and cloaks, beige-coloured lisle stockings, Harris Tweed jackets and beige brimmed hats, and walked in crocodile formation to the chapel at the ninth-century Sherborne Abbey that dominates the town. They walked back to school for breakfast, and returned to the abbey for 11 a.m. service. After lunch it was scripture prep for an hour, followed by writing letters home. After tea another service was held in the school hall. Miss Stuart was an impressive preacher who

delivered sermons at Evening Service, which the girls had to
attend. Scripture was an important part of the curriculum
and formed part of Helen Davidson's final examinations. The
playing field taught the girls lessons of corporate action with
no time for gossip or narrow-mindedness, which was apparently the bane of being a woman then. The school represented
a fine balance of learning, sport and recreation. The impact
of weather on outdoor sports was often severe. If low temperatures persisted, making normal games impossible, then
ice-skating on the lake in the grounds of the picturesque ruins
of the twelfth-century Sherborne Castle, south east of the
town, flourished.

Times for many people were hard in the early 1930s;
during Britain's most profound depression of the twentieth
century the unemployed numbered 3.5 million. But in 1931
Amy Johnson, the daring, pioneering English aviatrix, flew in
to Sherborne school as part of a fundraising exercise for the
planned new swimming pool there. It was another world. In
August 1934 Helen, aged 16 years 8 months, having applied
for a scholarship and place at the London School of Medicine
for Women, left Sherborne and attended a finishing school in
Switzerland for one year.

I turned my attention, for some time, to Alan Davidson
hoping to find more clues about Helen's background. But
after months of research I was finding biographical information on him was thin on the ground. He made a handwritten
will in 1923, curiously misspelling his first name twice, leaving
everything to his wife Sybil. When he filled in his daughter
Helen's scholarship application form he gave his address in
Putney and his profession as 'Director' – not much there. And
I found one mention of him in *The Times*: an obituary following his death, at 91, in April 1966 in Wimbledon hospital.

It was oddly lacking in detail, made no mention of his business life or family, and mainly praised his accomplishments as a figure skating champion of Great Britain in the English Style, a style which appealed mainly to adults who wanted something demanding and exciting without venturing into jumps and spins. Skating on frozen lakes was an aristocratic leisure pursuit at a time when tall black hats and black coats were de rigueur. In 1932 Alan Davidson was mainly responsible for merging the Wimbledon and Regents Park Skating Clubs to form the exclusive Royal Skating Club of which he was a member. The club, for which he had been honorary secretary and treasurer, had an elite membership of around twenty, whose secret, surviving files were closed until 2033 at The National Archives but recently opened at my request from their 100-year closure. It is apparent from those files that Alan Davidson was top drawer, mixing with aristocracy, politicians and royalty. Its list of members included HM George V, HRH Princess Mary, HM King Gustav of Sweden, HRH Princess Louise, Duchess of Argyll, HRH Duke of Connaught, Right Hon Viscount Simon who had been home secretary, foreign secretary, chancellor of the exchequer and lord chancellor, and Air Chief Marshall Lord Dowding. The club badge, which had to be worn when skating on club ice, was a silver skating boot. In 1933 Alan Davidson was made vice chairman of the National Skating Association. After searching through the Royal Skating Club files I discovered figure skating ran in the Davidson family. Anthony, Helen's older brother, was winning competition medals in the 1930s; in 1937 Helen was also admitted to the club as a Class A member. Included in the small, select group of ladies with whom she skated was Lady Patricia Ramsay, Queen Victoria's daughter who lived at St James's Palace.

Bit by bit I built up a picture. Helen's father Alan, born 1876 and his two elder brothers Nigel George, born 1873, and William Dalzell, born 1871, were sons of Alexander Davidson whose fortune had been built on gold mining in Australia, and the production of wrapping papers and packaging products in Great Britain. C Davidson and Sons Ltd of Mugiemoss in Scotland and London, established in 1876, had become the largest paper bag manufacturer in Britain. Alexander Davidson and his family lived on The Ridgway in the affluent area of Wimbledon populated by London's gentry, in the historic parish of Merton in South West London. Their grand residence in a wide residential street near Wimbledon Common was a sign of their wealth and success. Alexander died in 1920, after being knocked down by a car. All three boys were former Gownboys, one of the boarding houses at Charterhouse School in Godalming in the heart of the Surrey countryside, one of the seven great public schools of Britain – the others being Eton, Harrow, Winchester, Rugby, Westminster and Clifton. The Davidson brothers were upper class, rich, powerful and mixed in London's aristocratic circles. Their credentials as members of England's ruling class were impressive: Alan went up to Cambridge in 1894 and gained a Football Association Blue at a time when football was very much an upper-class sport (the rules of the game were largely drafted by students belonging to the university). He played centre forward for Cambridge in 1897 and gained a degree in Mathematics. Nigel Davidson went up to New College, Oxford, took a second class in Mods and Greats and represented Oxford in lawn tennis. William Davidson also went up to Oxford, to Magdalen College.

I emailed the archives at Charterhouse School as well as the assistant archivist and manuscript cataloguer at Trinity College,

Cambridge. From there I found more information about Alan
Davidson. He had business connections in the mining towns
of South Africa and was a director of African City Properties
Trust. From 1909 to 1919, he was company secretary for Eley
Brothers Ltd, manufacturers of firearms and cartridges. Later,
in secret files at The National Archives, I discovered Davidson
was in personal contact with the Secretary of State for War, a
British Cabinet-level position then, and found records of every
communication sent between the War Office, the Ministry of
Munitions and Eley Bros, who had been accused of supplying
dangerously defective, unserviceable .303 cartridges for government contracts, before and during the First World War. Eley
Bros responded to the criticism by stating their cartridges had
been made in accordance to War Office specification and had
passed all the necessary tests. The files also contained numerous
letters of complaint from the governor and commander in
chief, Malta; Brevet Colonel Graham, commanding the troops,
West Africa; the prime minister of Queensland concerning the
inferior quality of the ammunition supplied by the War Office;
and from the acting governor general of the Sudan.

The end of the hostilities on 11 November 1918 had brought
joy and relief with undertones of grief and a sense of loss.
Germany had been crushed but the full cost to Britain had still
to be calculated. Three quarters of a million young British men
had perished on battlefields; 1.5 million had been disabled or
damaged. Legions of ex-servicemen in Britain displayed their
medals whilst begging on street corners. The hunger marches
were soon to begin. In the summer of 1919, Alan Davidson,
now a director of Eley Bros, and in between winning trophies
in world championship ice-skating tournaments, left London
with his wife Sybil for Liverpool. Two year-old Helen and her
brother Anthony, 6, were left in the hands of the family's nanny

in London. On 9 August, the Davidsons boarded Cunard's Royal Mail Ship *Caronia* on a transatlantic business trip bound for New York. On the ship's list of passengers Alan Davidson had registered his occupation as 'film editor' and Sybil as a housewife. By the time they returned to England in October that year Davidson had been voted on to the board of directors of the Hudson Bay Company. Curiously, on their return voyage, he was registered on the passenger list as an engineer.

I searched for what might already be in the public domain about Nigel Davidson, and spent time leafing through leather-bound Foreign Office Lists at The National Archives, containing biographical information about Foreign Office employees, and also Charterhouse archives. Eventually I found proof of his official status as a leading figure in British diplomacy at the highest level in the Middle East. He was called to the Bar in 1899; civil judge and land registrar in Khartum, 1907; judicial adviser, Iraq Government, 1921; counsellor to the high commissioner of Iraq 1923; acting high commissioner 1924; legal secretary to the Sudan Government 1926–30. He was knighted in 1930 and retired from the diplomatic service but retained his links to it as a member of the Athenaeum Club in London, which with its connections to the Royal Society was at the heart of the English establishment. In 1931, in recognition of valuable advice to His Majesty King Faisal of Egypt, he was awarded the Order of the Nile. He was a director of Bilbao River and Cantabrian Railway, the Prudential Assurance Company and the British Mutual Banking Company. Between 1937 and 1961 he belonged to a 'Government Body'.

In October 1935, when her scholarship of £20 a year for four years came through, Helen Davidson went up to the London School of Medicine for Women to train to become a doctor. The estimated cost of a five-year medical degree course amounted to about £1,500. The red-brick-built school in Hunter Street in Brunswick Square was later renamed the London (Royal Free Hospital) Medical School for Women and was the only hospital in London at the time to offer clinical instruction to women. Women had made big strides in medicine during the First World War but afterwards their contribution to the health of the nation was not encouraged, except as nurses. Helen had dreamed of becoming a doctor since childhood and fought for it against the wishes of her mother who had tried to dissuade her. Women in those days who wanted careers did not get married. It was a clear case of career or marriage. Women grew up knowing their main role was to be a mother and homemaker. It was not only the responsibilities of caring for a family that fuelled objections to married women in the workplace; there were reservations about a woman's 'proper role' and that women would undercut men's wages and take their jobs. However, not many women went into the profession for money. Some were politically motivated, feminists, fighting for their rights. Some just wanted to be doctors. Many, like Helen, had to contend with opposition from their families. But Helen was prepared to give up on marriage and a family, detach herself from all relationships, defy tradition and was strong-minded enough to go against the wishes of her parents. She was determined to enter the world of medicine, known for its lack of opportunities for women, and would train to become a doctor during the war years.

Dr Brenda Sanderson, a fellow student of Helen Davidson at the London School of Medicine for Women and now in her 90s, remembers Helen: 'Helen was a top of the year student, a pretty girl with dark hair and blue eyes. She was older than many of the other girls and worked hard.' Dr Sanderson remembered that both of Helen's parents worked which was very unusual. What another student remembered vividly was the first day of human body dissection:

> I don't think I had a very comfortable night, the night before. Dressed in our long white coats we went up into the room called the Long Room, the name given to the anatomy dissection room. Inside there were two rows of dead bodies on slabs, five each side of the room, shrouded with white sheets, each student being allocated a part of a body. We had done a bit of dissection in biology at school and we calmly tried to prepare ourselves to cut up corpses. There were eight students and we would be doing limbs only. There would be two students on each arm and two on each leg. Then someone said, 'Go on, pull off the sheet'. We all looked at each other. Helen Davidson would have done the same. She would have been confronted with the shrouds. So we took off the sheet and looked the other way. It was absolutely incredible. We got very involved with the woman whose body we were using. She had a lovely history. It was good of her to leave her body to medical science – quite something.

Although Helen couldn't know it, this would be her fate twenty-six years later. She would be another body on a slab.

In 1938, having passed her second MD at the London School of Medicine, she entered the Royal Free Hospital in Grays Inn Road as a student. The number on her ticket was 2,904. There she began clinical studies, attended lectures and went on to do ward rounds with a consultant. She was allocated patients and learnt how to take a long patient history to sharpen her clinical skills. That year, according to the Royal Free Hospital Archives in Hampstead where I spent a day trawling through old records, Helen won the Winifred Secretan Patch Prize in anatomy. By July, as the nightmare of the German bombings in London was going on around her – nearly all the Royal Free's windows were blown in, air-raid casualties were being treated – Helen Davidson prepared to go into her final academic year. According to her medical school record her attendance at forensic, obstetrics and gynaecology lectures was disrupted with the bombing. She probably wondered if she would finish her studies. She learnt how to administer anaesthetics. It was very common for young doctors with little experience to be let loose on patients. Doctors were thrown in at the deep end. They would have used ethyl chloride sprayed on gauze and put over the patient's mouth; quantities were mainly an inspired guess. There were no intravenous injections then. During the winter term of 1939–40, Helen studied clinical psychiatry at Horton Psychiatric Hospital, near Epsom in Surrey. There were no psychiatric beds at the Royal Free Hospital then.

With her studies in the male-dominated world of medicine completed in April 1941, Helen Davidson graduated from London University as MB (Bachelor of Medicine) BS (Bachelor of Surgery). I spent hours trying to extract nuggets of information about her early medical career. Eventually I found a reference to a hardback volume called *Three Counties Hospital 1860–1960*, which mentioned the Three Counties Emergency Hospital in Arlesey, near St Albans, where Helen first practised as house physician. The hospital, previously a mental institution, had been requisitioned by the Health Authority for treating war casualties and had an arrangement with newly qualified students from the London School of Medicine. There had been a steady flow of patients to Arlesey where the work of doctors and nurses from the London School of Medicine was fully appreciated.

Towards the end of the Second World War, according to the BMA Medical Register, Helen Davidson's address was 77 Eaton Place, an expensively elegant, stone-clad eighteenth-century terrace in London's Belgravia, one of the most opulent areas of London. (The street featured prominently in the famous British TV drama *Upstairs Downstairs*.) Number 77, which Helen shared with her parents Alan and Sybil Davidson, had been divided into apartments, worth over £3 million in today's money. In the 1940s many residences formed a select enclave of embassies, offices relating to the war effort, the Foreign Office, home to important foreign refugees, and occupied by lords and ladies, all of whom were close to the heart of the British government. Lord North, flag officer in command of the North Atlantic station based in Gibralter, President Raczkiewicz of Poland and the Polish government in exile, the Swedish Embassy, the Austria Office and the Arab Office, the Belgian minister of finance, titled aristocracy, members of parliament, and peers of the realm typified the residents of this select street. The Davidsons lived exactly opposite Valentine Vivian, then head of the Secret Intelligence Services (SIS) and in charge of all counter-espionage operations. Vivian later approved the recruitment of British spy Kim Philby into the British Secret Service.

Alan's brother Nigel Davidson and Vivian had been long-standing colleagues since their bridge-playing Colonial Office days in the Middle East. They were deeply involved with the League of Nations mandate after the First World War, through which Britain and France would rule the Middle East, and with the establishment of the state of Iraq, previously known as Mesopotamia. Oil in the Middle East was becoming as desirable a resource as uranium became after the Second World War. Nigel Davidson was closely associated with Kim Philby's father whilst in the Middle East.

Lord Curzon, 5th Earl Howe who lived at number 41 was a British naval officer and retired MP. He was a tall, slim man of aristocratic appearance but privately he was quiet and shy. There was an irony in that Howe became a well-known racing driver taking the sport up seriously at the age of 44. He co-founded the British Racing Drivers' Club. His father, the Rt Hon George Nathaniel Curzon, had been viceroy and governor general of India. Earl Howe's ancestral home, along with a substantial surrounding estate, was Penn House in Penn Street, outside Amersham. He always had a strong connection with the town.

As the war ploughed on to its last days Helen moved out of London, away from Eaton Place where she had mixed with people with power and influence, leaving behind a city of widespread ruin. She arrived in the small provincial town of Old Amersham as a young, single woman beginning her career in general practice with Dr Johns and Dr Rolt at their surgery, an imposing double-fronted Georgian house called The Firs in the high street. Helen moved into lodgings in an elegant three-storey Georgian house called The White House in Church Street, a narrow, quiet street with long front gardens, and facing St Mary's church. It was at the northern edge of the town where it becomes countryside. This was a time when big changes were being made in health care. Before 1948, when the National Health Service was born, you paid for health care, relied on charity or went without.

From the Royal Skating Club files, I found that in 1946 Alan and Sybil Davidson moved from Eaton Place to Acacia House in Mortlake, a fine Georgian property of historic interest six miles from Hyde Park Corner. It backed on to the south bank of the River Thames, close to the finishing line of the annual Oxford and Cambridge University Boat Race.

7

Seeing the Wood for the Trees: November 1966

One person who knew Hodgemoor Wood intimately was David Mulkern. In woodland, bordering Phil Pearce's fields, opposite Stockings Farm in Bottrells Lane, he worked as a charcoal burner. He lived there, worked there; he knew every path and probably every tree. He had been making charcoal in the woodlands since the late 1950s and over the years had been featured in newspaper articles and on a BBC television documentary about his occupation:

Hodgemoor Wood in 1966 was a vast jungle, almost impenetrable woodland and scrub. There were no proper tracks. Access had been more or less unrestricted, apart from the fact that it was overgrown. It bears no resemblance now to what it was like then. It was three times as dense, overgrown, and there'd been no proper tree clearing. The tracks that horses used were not proper horses' tracks, just trails left by the odd tractor. To give you an idea of what it was like – after the murder of Dr Davidson we had a mobile home on site and were constantly getting people coming in, lost, asking where they were.

Mr Mulkern had occupied his current site on an abandoned Second World War sewerage works since 1963, after the Forestry Commission had moved him off his original spot 100 yards further back in the woodland:

In 1963 I got a contract from the Forestry Commission to clear the wood. Whatever they wanted burned, we burned. They decided what needed coppicing and we would coppice. Quite soon afterwards, one of the residents of Chalfont St Giles, the village at the eastern end of Bottrells Lane, brought out a High Court injunction stopping the Forestry Commission from cutting any more trees down. The felling was upsetting the residents and walkers from walking their dogs. The injunction stopped us cutting trees pending consideration of the future management plan for the woodland. It was at that point I was forced to move off my site. I had to move all five wood burning kilns to the derelict bit of land by the sewerage works and clear and concrete the area. In turn the Commission stopped me burning. They never refunded me for the loss of the contract. It was supposed to be on a temporary basis until the injunction was settled. I'd been charcoal burning there since my mid-twenties, mainly on my own, sometimes with my brother-in-law, but I never went back to the original site in the wood.

Having landed the contract to clear the area, suddenly I was out of work and had to find work elsewhere to tide me over. The Forestry Commission promised alternative sites. It came to nothing. I only obtained areas in the woodland piecemeal, nothing I could rely on. We had five kilns on the site and my livelihood depended on the woods. It meant I had to bring timber in from outside using a tractor and trailer. I usually got waste wood from sawmills near Beaconsfield – whatever they were cutting, mainly big slabs of semi-round tree trunks from oak.

It was a complicated time in the woodland's history. Around 70–80 per cent of British timber was cut down during the Second World War for the war effort. By the 1960s, it was a case of restocking the forests. The Forestry Commission was concentrating its efforts into converting unproductive beech woods into a profitable enterprise by planting acres of quick growing spruce. But their activities in wholesale felling of hardwoods and replanting with conifers had, as Mr Mulkern told me, produced storms of protest as I also discovered from secret Forestry Commission files at The National Archives. The newly formed Hodgemoor Woods Association wanted tighter control on development in the woodland, arguing that Hodgemoor Wood was public open space. The general public had no idea of the row over the ownership of the forest between Buckinghamshire County Council, the Forestry Commission and the Hodgemoor Wood Association or about the wholesale destruction of the woods. The three organisations were fighting it out: profit versus amenity. The fact that these files, interweaving the problems in the woods with Dr Davidson's murder in 1966, were closed until 1995 was interesting. The murder brought matters to a head. Tree felling in the forest was halted for another six months, and with detectives leaning over Mr Mulkern's charcoal kilns during the murder investigation, what was left of his work was considerably slowed up.

If retired police officer Tony Dale had not mentioned to me that the weapon used to kill Dr Davidson was a three-foot length of burnt poplar wood, I would have missed it. The species of wood had not been specified in any newspaper report at the time of the police investigation. I recalled the interview with Dale when he told me about the murder weapon:

> I always remember it was poplar because I never knew what a poplar tree looked like. There were lots of bits of timber lying around, not stacked, burnt remains of wood clearance after felling of some poplars. My recollection is that there was a delay in finding it. It had been picked up close to the immediate scene of crime. I do not know who by. The forensic scientist told us a few days later it was poplar. It was common knowledge at the police station. It was no secret. It would have been carefully retained as an exhibit.

It wasn't until I came across articles in local newspapers marking the anniversaries of the doctor's murder that I found any reports specifying poplar wood. From Dale's perspective it was common knowledge that the presumed murder weapon was a length of poplar. It is odd therefore that this detail never made the papers at the time. Was it intentionally omitted from press briefings? Why did it only reach the public domain in 1986 when Dale recounted the story for an article in the *Bucks Free Press* on the twentieth anniversary of Dr Davidson's murder? He was also quoted in the 1996 and 2006 editions of the same newspaper marking the thirtieth and fortieth anniversaries, saying, 'A bloody piece of wood was found close to her body. It was a piece of poplar.'

I remembered my interview with the late forensic pathologist Professor David Bowen who allowed me to read his personal copy of the post-mortem report on Helen Davidson, and a letter to him, dated 16 November 1966, from Det Ch Insp Napier at the Metropolitan Police Forensic Science Laboratory. Napier suggested a meeting to see the 'large piece of burnt wood found at the scene'. There was no mention of poplar in this official documentation. Napier asked Dr Bowen if he would like to see the wood, and asked him to telephone to arrange an appointment. For some reason Dr Bowen did not reply to the letter.

The police photographer Det Con John Bailey was not asked by Det Ch Sup Williams or Det Insp Napier to photograph the length of poplar, the presumed murder weapon. David Mulkern was unaware that the alleged murder weapon was a piece of poplar. When I told him he replied, 'That's strange. I can't recall seeing any poplar in the wood. I would be very surprised if it had grown there. Poplar certainly was not the sort of wood that grows in mixed woodland. It's the wrong sort of situation. I'm surprised the police knew what it was.' He added, 'If it wasn't a fir tree they wouldn't have any idea.'

Poplar of any variety was not a timber suitable for charcoal production. Mr Mulkern summed up the reasons:

It's 70–80 per cent water, and being full of moisture burns unevenly. The more moisture in the wood, the more wood you're burning away. It is not something a charcoal burner would use. My customers wouldn't have accepted it. The wood for charcoal needs to be coppiced. That means they're regularly cut to ground level in order to make them grow quickly, so they regenerate quickly for another crop. You can see lots of coppicing stools in the wood where it has been cut again and again. Chestnut is favourite with beech second.

I asked if poplar wood could have been taken into the woodland. 'Local contractors who wanted to get rid of trees could have brought it in to the woodlands to burn it.'

I looked at the facts. I felt something was missing. According to official documents from 1966, the Forestry Commission had given a precise list of woodland trees and shrubs in Hodgemoor Wood. The wood was made up of oak standards, beech, sweet chestnut, hornbeam, ash, hazel, birch, dense thorn, scrub and bracken. Poplar was not included in the list. The charcoal burner said poplar could have been taken there to be burnt by a gardening contractor. A length of poplar had been used as a murder weapon. I could not find one reference to poplar wood in any newspaper article at the time of the murder hunt even though it was common knowledge at Amersham police station. It should be in the police reports that the Major Crime Review Team at Thames Valley Police will not allow me to see. Why didn't the newspapers publish this information? Had the police not mentioned it in their early morning press briefings during the murder inquiry? The species of wood was eventually reported many years later in interviews that Dale had given to local newspapers in connection with the murder.

What bothered me was that the picture I got from Dale's recollections that 'poplar had been growing there, had been cut down, and there were other pieces of timber lying around but not stacked – burned remains of wood clearances after felling of some poplars' didn't match David Mulkern's testimony about the make-up of the woodland, the information about the injunction that had halted work in the woods, and the Forestry Commission's exact list of trees and shrubs growing in Hodgemoor then. Dale admitted the length of wood was not found immediately and he did not witness its retrieval. There was a gap of about forty-eight hours between the discovery of the body on 10 November, and the finding of the length of bloodstained timber. Shortly before lunchtime on Saturday 12 November, two days after the body was found, Rosalind and Phil Pearce from Stockings Farm, and their neighbours Lloyd King and his daughter Hilary from Meadow Cottage, visited the crime scene out of curiosity. Rosalind Pearce said:

> It was almost like a clearing, not much bigger than twelve feet in diameter. We saw sticky blood spatters, roughly at shoulder height over the trees surrounding where the body had lain. There was no police officer guarding the site. Detectives later told us that the murderer would have been covered in blood because of the amount that had splashed around over a wide area.

Dale had said, 'It was thought the length of wood was the murder weapon because of the blood.' I reconsidered the letter dated 16 November 1966, six days after the body was found, from Det Insp Napier at the Metropolitan Police Forensic Science Laboratory to Dr Bowen, the forensic pathologist who carried out the post-mortem on Helen Davidson. Napier wrote that 'the large piece of burnt wood found at the scene gives a strong reaction for blood, and examination is being made to try and identify the pieces of charcoal found in the wound with this piece of wood'. He had focused on the charcoal. More to the point, why did he not check if the blood on the presumed murder weapon matched the blood that had been spattered on surrounding trees during the attack on Helen Davidson? This could have confirmed the length of timber was the murder weapon. It is clear from the list of exhibits taken possession of at the scene of the crime, and recorded in Napier's letter to Dr Bowen, that blood samples had not been taken from the surrounding trees.

A retired Flying Squad forensic scientist who cannot be named commented:

> A strong reaction for blood forty years ago means the scientist couldn't even identify if the blood was human. He would have needed to elaborate as to why in his opinion the reason for the strong reaction, and why no further attempts to identify the 'ownership' of the blood were made. In the interim period between the finding of the body and the finding of the length of timber it could easily have become contaminated with blood from woodland animals. It could have been badger blood. This should have been obvious to the police. The forensic scientist should have been pressed about the blood.

Det Ch Supt Williams, Scotland Yard's chief investigating officer, spent the first few hours, then days and weeks, focusing on the chance killing of Dr Davidson, a woman with no enemies, and that the killing was motiveless. He was not open to any other theory. He had boxed himself in with assumptions. As a result he got no leads, he did not find the killer and the investigation came to a dead end.

What may have looked like a chance murder to the police had taken on a new dimension for me. It was more complicated than the police thought. They didn't see what was in front of their noses. According to the police the woods had been the subject of tree thinning, the waste poplar wood subsequently being burnt in bonfires. Did they not realise that the High Court injunction had halted the felling of trees and making bonfires? The police jumped to conclusions about the burnt wood, had not scrutinised or questioned the poplar's origins and had not considered alternative scenarios. From the evidence, it would be easy to deduce that the poplar wood had been brought into the woodland by a contractor, possibly employed in garden maintenance, who was burning his waste timber illegally. Had the police not thought that the bonfires might be connected with the killer? Had they misjudged the evidence found in the woodland? Had the doctor disturbed someone who enjoyed making bonfires? An arsonist? The police had not looked at the scene of the crime from those perspectives. It was in a small clearing that the attacker by chance came across the doctor and killed her. That was the official police story reported in the press.

When Helen Davidson reached the clearing in Hodgemoor Wood, a confined space no bigger than twelve foot in diameter, the killer was already holding a three-foot piece of burnt timber in his hand, which he must have previously picked up some distance from the crime scene. Then, as she lay on her back on the ground the attacker trampled Helen's eyes into her skull with a shod foot: the action of a killer who knew his victim well. It could not have been the sudden unpremeditated attack assumed by Det Ch Supt Williams.

Early on in the murder investigation, senior local police officers told the Pearce family at Stockings Farm a very different story. They were sure this wasn't a random murder and that Dr Davidson knew or recognised her attacker. Rosalind Pearce said:

The police went on looking for a murder weapon for a couple of weeks. In addition to the infamous 'lump of wood' they continued to look for something else for some time. I seem to remember they searched some water. And as I recall, pretty much the only water in that wood was a small pond directly behind the charcoal burners' yard. One of our neighbours looking out of an upstairs bedroom window at Brentford Grange Farm also saw a line of approximately fifty police officers walking side by side across the fields near our home which was quite a way from Hodgemoor Wood. They were obviously still looking for a murder weapon.

8

The Housekeeper at Hyde Heath

Rosalind Pearce's observations were correct. The police were continuing their search for a weapon, but not only in Hodgemoor Wood. They had taken a particular interest in, and were carrying out a thorough check of, the bungalow called Rosemead, Kathleen Cook's home in Hyde Heath, a village five miles away from the scene of the murder. In public, Det Ch Supt Jack Williams was saying that: Helen Davidson's binoculars, through which she had spied illicit lovers, indirectly led to her death; she was a woman with no enemies; it was highly unlikely she would have been followed to the wood for a premeditated attack; and a piece of burnt wood about three feet long found near the murder scene had been identified as the murder weapon. But behind the scenes the police were following a new line of enquiry. They had been alerted to a suspicious connection between Helen Davidson and her cleaning lady, Herbert Baker's former housekeeper Kathleen Cook. Few cars ever passed through Hyde Heath, so the unexpected sight of police cars parked on the wide grass verge beside the quiet lane running through the village, and uniformed police officers carrying shovels and digging up the front garden at Rosemead on a grey winter's day, was very unusual.

Rob Stevens lived next door to Rosemead in a house called Penhurst. He said, 'Kathleen's house was searched by the police for the murder weapon. The back and front gardens were dug up as well.' This one clue sparked my curiosity. It led me away from Hodgemoor Wood and the assumed murder weapon to a possible motive for Dr Davidson's murder.

In a road of modest and large well-kept properties, in the 1960s, Rosemead in Weedon Hill, was scruffy. Lying twenty yards back from the road and only just visible by passers-by, the property looked as though it hadn't been touched in years. Its overgrown front garden ensured no one was welcome. This dilapidated bungalow, about a quarter of a mile from the centre of the village, was the house in which Dr Davidson had attended Herbert Baker's invalid first wife Ruby, until her death in 1960 at the age of 70. When Herbert married Dr Davidson in September 1961, and moved to live at Ashlyn in Chesham Bois, he left his house in the hands of Kathleen Cook.

How does Kathleen fit into this story? I had already established that at the time of the doctor's death, Kathleen lived alone in the bungalow. She cleaned for the doctor at Ashlyn in Chesham Bois once a week. She kept herself to herself. She attended church twice on Sunday mornings, firstly at the Baptist Chapel in Brays Lane at 9.30 a.m. then on to the tiny church of St Andrews for the later service where she sang in the choir. She was often visited during the week by Herbert Baker. She had spent thirty years in service for Herbert and his late wife and a strong bond had been forged between them.

The police had heard about the relationship between Herbert and Kathleen. According to Det Sgt Tony Dale, Kathleen who had hoped to win Mr Baker after the death of his first wife Ruby was jealous of Helen Davidson's marriage to him. She had set her sights on the wealthy, elderly man and Helen had taken him away from her. There could not have been more of a contrast in the two women's backgrounds. They were miles apart socially and the animosity between them was obvious. Kathleen started life in the workhouse and was fostered. Her unimportant life of hardship didn't match that of Helen's with her connections, great opportunities and a family that moved in aristocratic circles. Kathleen had no reason to be fond of the doctor. She had cause to hate her.

Helen Davidson was a woman of habit and Kathleen Cook, more than anyone, would have known the doctor's weekly routine: her regular Wednesday afternoons off when she exercised her dog in the countryside and went birdwatching, and Thursdays and Fridays when she practised as an anaesthetist at Chesham Cottage Hospital. Kathleen was also one of the only people who could handle Fancy, Helen Davidson's snappy, anti-social wire-haired terrier, who only liked being with people he knew. For years Kathleen Cook, a plain-looking woman of short stature, with dark hair and glasses had lived virtually unnoticed. My investigation enabled me to reconstruct her unimportant life of hardship, and with scant details unearthed in a local history archive I began to unravel Kathleen's sad story.

Kathleen Louise Cook was born in 1922 into a poor family. Her parents, Winifred and James Cook, lived in a cottage in Swan Yard in the large village of Hanslope, now part of the Borough of Milton Keynes. Kathleen's childhood changed forever with the Depression in the 1920s when so many were

still struggling to recover from the First World War. Life was
harsh. James Cook, a farm labourer, fell out of work. The
family's cottage had become dilapidated. Things mounted into
a disaster. The only recourse then for the unemployed living
in utter destitution, and too poor to maintain themselves, was
the dreaded workhouse. In the mid-1920s the whole family
was taken into the Union Workhouse in Newport Pagnell.
Shortly afterwards Kathleen and her younger sister Dorothy,
born in 1924, were taken away from their parents to live with
foster parents. Mr and Mrs Cook never saw their daughter
Kathleen again. Fostering for her must have left a psychological scar. Her childhood had been lost. She grew up knowing
that her parents, who had sent her forty-four miles away from
Newport Pagnell to be fostered in Hyde Heath, had betrayed
her. Travelling that distance now is easy. In the 1920s, however,
it was a long trek, further than 9-year-old Kathleen had ever
travelled in her life before.

The 1920s is a blank now to nearly all Hyde Heath villagers
except for one 90 year old, Mrs Irma Dolphin. She was an
early settler from London and has lived in Hyde Heath almost
her entire life. She is probably the only person who remembers the village when Kathleen Cook first moved there to be
fostered by Mr and Mrs Eldridge:

> In those days it really was rural, no more than a handful
> of houses and bungalows, two shops, a bakery, the Post
> Office, a school, chapel, church and five farms. You could
> stroll down Brays Lane and see pigs and cows watching you
> from behind hawthorn hedges. There was no electricity
> and only a small population. There were cherry orchards
> and the cottages around the common with no inside toilets
> were occupied by farm workers. Village people who had

to work usually became gardeners, farm workers or went into domestic service at what were called the big houses. Anyone who travelled out of the village to work was considered a cut above the rest.

Fostering, known then as boarding out, was a lucrative source of weekly income, a practice not necessarily pursued out of love for children. Ernest William Eldridge and his wife Annie lived in a small semi-detached Victorian cottage called Fairview in Weedon Hill. They were strict Baptists having married at the Lower Baptist Chapel in Amersham and had no children of their own. Annie always dressed in long, black dresses that made her look old. She was the archetypal foster mother of the early twentieth century, who fostered children of all ages, coping with them using strictness. She was of average height, very upright, matronly and rarely smiled. Ernest was a carpenter by trade. Outwardly he was a devout member of the chapel in Brays Lane. Behind closed doors he was a brutal foster father who regularly whipped and beat foster children in his care. Kathleen had been living with the Eldridges for a short while when Ernest died suddenly in 1932 of heart failure at the age of 63, leaving his wife Annie to bring up the foster children single-handed. She was not well off but she was house-proud and got the fostered children to do most of the work around the house. There was no indoor lavatory, no mains water and no piped water into the kitchen. The only place to wash was at the kitchen sink, with water obtained by hand pump from a well in the garden.

'We came to the village in 1927,' said Irma Dolphin:

I was at school with Kathleen Cook. First at Hyde Heath primary then at White Hill Senior Girls School in Chesham, from 11 to 14 years of age. She was a strange person and lived with Gran Eldridge her very strict foster mother. Children at the primary school knew somehow that Kathleen was not really one of them. She had not shared her early childhood with other children, was not allowed to mix at school and wasn't liked much. She had even less in common with girls at senior school. We used to go together on the bus. When we got to Chesham she'd race up the hill to get to school first at nine o'clock when the bell rang while we sauntered up. Miss Morrison, the headmistress, a very strict Scots woman used to say 'If Kathleen Cook can get here on time, so can you.' She did her utmost to get into everyone's good books. She was the only girl who had 100 per cent for conduct at school, which was weird. She was rather quiet, very religious and went to Chapel on a Sunday morning and to St Andrews Church of England straightaway afterwards. I used to think it was a double indemnity to make sure she went to heaven.

With Gran Eldridge, Kathleen learnt the skills of housekeeping. As a young teenager she almost ran the house. She was capable and was allowed to supervise the preparation of meals for the smaller children. When she left school at the age of 14, she was taken straight into service by Mr and Mrs Baker as a cook and general help at Rosemead about 100 yards up the road, later becoming housekeeper when Mrs Baker became bedridden with arthritis. 'Mr Baker was working in London at the time,' said Mrs Dolphin. 'He always looked smart when he was in his work clothes and around the village he doffed his cap to other people in his class. He was always well respected. I can recall him pushing Ruby out in a wheelchair then.' During the 1950s Irma remembers seeing Kathleen driving

Bob and Fennis Marston in the 1960s. (Bob Marston)

Maria Marston in 2013. (Maria Marston)

Dr Helen Davidson. (Source unknown)

London School of Medicine for Women. (Royal Free Hospital Archives)

Ashlyn, Dr Davidson's house in Chesham Bois. (Author's photo)

Dr Davidson (second from right) and Herbert Baker (second row, third from left) at Amersham Choral Society. (Rosie Woodfall)

Amersham Bus Garage, 1956. (Richard Proctor)

Amersham police station in the early 1960s. (Tony Dale)

Amersham police station staff, early 1960s. Det Sgt Tony Dale standing far right.
(Tony Dale)

Michael Larcombe. (Michael Larcombe)

Hyde Heath school. (Dennis Silcocks)

Police cadet, Brian Shirley, in the 1960s. (Brian Shirley)

Kathleen Cook (third from left) in 1987. (Irma Dolphin)

Anthony Garrett. (Felicity Garrett)

Hodgemoor Wood. (Author's photo)

Bottrells Lane. (Author's photo)

Det Con John Bailey, police photographer. (John Bailey)

The site of Dr Davidson's murder in Hodgemoor Wood. (Author's photo)

Stockings Farm, Bottrells Lane. (Author's photo)

Dr Davidson's body with her dog, Fancy, beside her. (Source unknown)

Professor David Bowen. (Author's photo)

Helen Davidson's grave. (Author's photo)

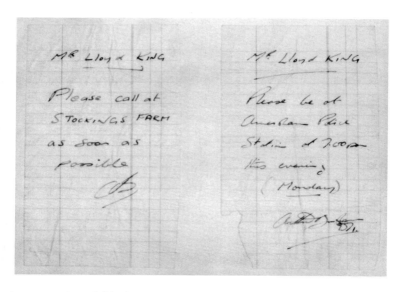

Notes left by the police for Lloyd King. (Joyce King's collection)

Gipsies on the Move

It is a hot day, and on a dusty country lane there are some gipsies. On such a day the horses find their caravans heavy, and they walk very slowly. The gipsies find it hot also, and they walk in what little shade there is, under the hedges, and beside the caravans. The children are tired, so they stop to have their mid-day meal, which consists of stew, ale, and biscuits. It is a hot day for stew, but they have it. They continue in the afternoon, and are glad when the evening dusk comes; even the children brighten up, and play with more zeal, and the gipsies talk to the horses, and among themselves. The horses seem to like being talked to, and patted, for they seem eager to please. The night is falling and the gipsies are in bed; the camp fire is dying out, and only glowing embers are left when the camp is sleeping.

HELEN DAVIDSON (Upper III.K.)

Essay by Helen Davidson, aged 12. (Putney High School)

Herbert Baker's black car around the village. Herbert had recently retired from his job as bank clerk in London. 'There was a garage beside the house in which he kept his car and he taught Kathleen to drive. It was long before the first Mrs Baker died. I knew he gave her lessons, I saw them driving together. I never saw her driving alone.'

Irma, as dressmaker to the local gentry, was employed to make comfortable nightgowns for Ruby Baker:

Mr Baker used to buy lovely soft material from London, which I would make up into nightdresses for Mrs Baker. I only stepped inside Rosemead twice: once to measure Ruby Baker for her new long nightgowns. She laid flat on the bed for this. She was a tall, thin-looking lady. Another time I went to the house to deliver finished items and saw from the kitchen into the bedroom where Mrs Baker was in bed.

Kathleen had a sheltered life and came from a poor background, so to be employed as a housekeeper to a wealthy old man would have been a good position and a big opportunity. A relationship with Herbert Baker would have been a step up on the social ladder. But between 1960 and 1961 Kathleen experienced a double bereavement. Ruby Baker, whom she had nursed for twenty-four years, died on 5 February 1960. Less than a year later Kathleen's foster mother Annie Eldridge, with whom she had lived since being abandoned as a young child, and whom she also nursed during a serious illness until her death, died in January 1961, aged 86.

For Kathleen her employer's marriage in September 1961 must have magnified her own insecurity and felt like another rejection. The life she had known was being taken away from her. It was understandable she should feel jealous and embittered. For her entire life Kathleen had been dependent on Herbert Baker. He had taught her to drive and she found the security she had craved. A month after Herbert and Helen's marriage, Kathleen was forced to move out of Fairfield, her home for the last thirty years. It was up for sale. She moved temporarily into another village house, but soon moved into Rosemead where she obviously thought she belonged.

She was never the same after Herbert's marriage to the doctor. The pattern of her life had been shaped by the first abandonment as a child and repeated by another rejection. She felt cut off from the life she'd carved for herself since the bad old days of the workhouse. Her foster parents were dead. Herbert whom she had hoped to win had gone too. She was envious of the doctor and resented this woman who had caused his affection to shift. The envy had an immediate effect. What had previously been untidiness at Rosemead became an obsession. People living in the village said she became something of a recluse cocooning herself at the house in a mass of cardboard boxes – probably a modicum of security from the outside world. Mrs Rob Stevens, the new young wife of her neighbour at Penhurst, was the only person other than the police, to ever enter Kathleen's home:

> She didn't have a fire. The entire space, but for a slither of a passage between the front door and the back window of the sitting room, was stacked with newspapers and cardboard boxes from floor to ceiling, wall to wall, from the back door through a little hall into the lounge which spanned the back of the house. A single chair and an electric fire stood in a clearing in the sitting room. The little path went back into the kitchen, absolutely awful, and it was the same

in the front room. Dust was an inch thick. It was all like this except for the mantelpiece. There were three wedding photographs, which were kept in pristine condition: one of my husband and me, her niece and husband in another and a couple I didn't recognise in the third. I don't know how they could be so clean.

Visitors were not invited in to the house. Gradually the garden became more overgrown. A tiny path wound through the bushes and trees grew up through the grass. It was like a sea of brambles. Kathleen liked it that way. One gentleman who delivered shopping to her home said she was like a little hermit. 'When she opened the door the inside looked the same as the outside, full of clutter. I didn't go in; I just deposited shopping on the doorstep. In Amersham you'd see her wandering around. She never seemed to be with anybody and never spoke to anybody.'

In most murders the victim knows the assailant. The people closest to the victim are always suspected or questioned certainly. But it was as if Kathleen didn't exist. There was no mention of her in the press. Yet she had motives. She hadn't been in service for nearly thirty years only to be upstaged by another woman after the death of Herbert's first wife.

Some people from the village in the 1960s described Kathleen as nondescript, of limited intelligence, defensive, withdrawn, never in the community, always on the fringe – phrase after phrase of derogatory comments about her. Perhaps 'more like repressed by the ruling class' was a kinder description. One elderly lady, whose family had been treated by Dr Davidson for four generations, couldn't believe Kathleen's visions of grandeur and looked down disapprovingly at her. 'Kathleen Cook thought Herbert Baker would marry her.

It was quite extraordinary! She didn't know her place. Ruby Baker, his first wife was *looked after* by Kathleen. She thought she was a nurse. She was not. She was a carer.' In her favour those who met her in the village said she was always clean and dressed neatly. And the one thing she could do well, most of the time, was keep Dr Davidson's dog under control.

Ann Honour, who moved to Hyde Heath in 1966, knew Herbert Baker and Kathleen. 'After the murder Kathleen looked after Dr Davidson's dog until he was quite an advanced age. She didn't take him out much. He was quite quirky and unsociable.' Ruth Groves, who had lived in the village since 1965, said Herbert Baker was quite a busy man with church commitments and didn't remember him being much of a dog walker. She recalled:

> I do not believe Fancy was of a very friendly disposition so I saw it very little. I think Kathleen was afraid it could be aggressive. She was always saying the dog was very unreliable and only liked being with people she knew. I can only assume such an animal would require more time invested than Herbert had time, or willingness, to devote to such a task. Perhaps this could be considered a part of Kathleen's recompense for living in Rosemead.

Local GP Dr Bryn Neale became neighbours with Kathleen Cook:

> When we moved into the village she was quite fearsome. We had three boys. Kathleen would come to the bottom of the garden and tell the boys her dogs would bite them. The gossip was that she had been bequeathed the house. She was a suspect for the murder. She was fond of Herbert Baker.

Could this relationship between Kathleen Cook and Herbert Baker be the key to unlocking Dr Davidson's murder? Were Kathleen's 'visions of grandeur' sufficient to motivate her into murder? Kathleen may have been 'of limited intelligence' but she was also a jealous woman, in desperate need of money and wanted revenge: three motives for murder. She also knew how to handle the doctor's dog.

The Amersham police force served 24,000 people in 1966 and covered an area of 17,000 acres. A team of forty or fifty police officers were involved in the murder hunt for Dr Davidson's killer. The post office in Brays Lane was at the centre of the police inquiry. Irma Dolphin recalled 'When the police were investigating the murder, the lady at the post office at the time gave the police a lot of help.' Det Sgt Tony Dale remembered:

Door to door enquiries were not confined to Amersham. They were extended to villages, mainly Seer Green, Chalfont St Giles, Coleshill, Hyde Heath. Enquiries were not specific to any particular age group. We didn't pull in all local criminals – not a thing we would do. We did question all those with convictions or suspicion of sexual offence although there was no indication of sexual offence involved. We were aware that peepers or flashers could be suspect. Several were given a grilling but all were alibi'd and could not be connected.

Michael Baughan, who lived three doors away from Kathleen Cook said, 'We were never questioned. The police never showed any interest, never came knocking on doors in Hyde Heath.' I asked Dale how thoroughly Kathleen Cook was questioned. 'I don't know who interviewed her but it would normally be by two police officers, one a WPC. I don't recall where Kathleen Cook was on the 9 November but I do know she was fully cleared of any involvement quite early in the enquiry.' Not that quickly it seems. Digging up Kathleen's front garden must have taken time and the police must have had their suspicions.

The 22 December 1966 edition of the *Buckinghamshire Advertiser* reported: 'MURDER HUNT POLICE SEARCH FOR NEW CLUES. Some members of the team are still re-checking the 500–600 statements taken during the hunt, in search of new clues.'

Few Hyde Heath people would speak to me directly about the rumours in the 1960s, which had spread round the village concerning Kathleen's involvement in the doctor's death. Even though murder was rare, many agreed they were too busy earning a living to get involved in the police enquiries, and were afraid of talking too much in case they got saddled with the murder. In the very secret lives of Hyde Heath's middle class, many were cagey about answering any questions giving the impression of a village with secrets. 'What happened to the old boy's money?' asked Ted Hance, the farmer that supplied Channel Islands milk to the dairy in Top Amersham where Dr Davidson was last seen on 9 November. 'It would be interesting to find out. Keep looking,' he said to me. Could money have been a motive for murder?

Did the police check Helen Davidson's will? Who would have benefitted from her death? Herbert Baker was the main beneficiary to her estate then valued at over £24,000. What did Kathleen have to gain? She would gain Herbert Baker, the love of her life, as well as a home, security and money. She had come a long way since the Newport Pagnell workhouse and was not happy seeing an inheritance drifting away from her with Herbert's marriage to Helen Davidson. When Baker died nine years later did the police check his will for beneficiaries? Were the police aware that Kathleen inherited the freehold of Rosemead after Herbert's death in 1975, all its effects and a legacy of £2,000? And contrary to what most locals said that they hadn't seen Kathleen drive a car and had only ever seen her walking or taking the bus from the point where it stopped, not far from Rosemead, Kathleen did in fact drive. In 1975 she also inherited Herbert Baker's car.

David Oxley was born in Hyde Heath. His father and brother were fostered by Annie Eldridge not long after the First World War. At about the age of 8, David visited Mrs Eldridge at Fairview in Weedon Hill with his father. He saw Kathleen Cook taking charge of the household, busying herself at meal times. He offered to tell me the following:

Dr Davidson became my doctor when I was about 7. She was a lovely, gentle person. As years went on this [the murder] faded into memory. It was only recently it started coming to light again. A person I know in Hyde Heath was talking to me. He said 'Do you know that little old bungalow that has just been sold for building?' He explained to me where it was. 'It's just been sold for a million pounds. A lot of money. That's where that murderess used to live.'

'I beg your pardon', I said.

'That woman who murdered Dr Davidson used to live there.'

'What ever are you talking about?' I said. 'That murder was never solved.'

'To be honest,' he continued, 'I wasn't around at the time. A lot of the villagers said that's who did the murder. What you don't know is I know the man's occupation that gave her the alibi. He said she was with him when Dr Davidson was murdered.'

I didn't say anything at the time but when I left him and I was on my way home I started to think about what he'd said. Because the lady who lived in Rosemead, I knew. I thought, you have to be joking, there's no way she could have done that. Her name was Kathleen [Cook]. After I'd spoken to this person in Hyde Heath I started putting two and two together. Was it an eternal triangle? It began to make a bit more sense. Not that I could even envisage Kathy killing anyone, but these things happen. As far as I know she never had a car. I never saw her driving. Hodgemoor Wood, the scene of the murder, was some miles from Hyde Heath. I found it difficult to believe she could batter someone to death. I've no idea who he was. He wouldn't tell me. From what I can gather Kathleen was very upset when Baker married Dr Davidson. Whether she was strong enough to have committed murder, I doubt it. But I do not doubt she could have been involved.

Was this 'triangle' the reason the police dug up Kathleen's garden? She did harbour a hatred for Helen Davidson. Did the police adequately check her alibi for 9 November 1966? According to one villager, Kathleen received 'a decidedly hard lot of dealings with the police'.

Arrows pointed at Kathleen Cook.

9

Mr Herbert Charles Baker

It was 13 November 1966, four days since the murder of Helen
Davidson. The assumption of the random killing by a person
unknown to the doctor continued in the newspapers, and the
police did not appear to be any closer to knowing who killed
her. But Herbert Baker went ahead with his plans to preach a
sermon at the Remembrance Day service at St Andrews church
in Hyde Heath where he was a lay reader. Instead of showing
signs of shock or disbelief about his wife's violent death, the
theme of his address that morning was forgiveness. He was
nearly 80 years old, frail-looking, and preached without any
display of emotion. He chose as his text 1 Corinthians 15:55:
'O death, where is thy sting? O grave, where is thy victory?' In
his sermon he told the twenty members of the congregation

> I selected these words about two months ago, but I little
> thought I would have such an immediate occasion to rely
> on them. The dark days will come when I shall miss my

dear wife and I shall be tempted to despair. But my Saviour
will be with me – I know he will not fail me.

He asked the congregation to feel no resentment or anger for
his wife's killer, but to join him in offering prayers. Perhaps it
was his way of dealing with loss and coming to terms with it.
Grief affects people in different ways. Conventions were different then. Having been married to his first wife Ruby for
forty-eight years, nursing her for the best part of their married
life, the brutal and sudden death of his second wife after just
five years of marriage must have been a shocking experience
for him especially at 79 years of age and being thrown into the
spotlight after years of privacy. But forgiveness was not what
others felt. No one else felt any mercy for the doctor's killer.
Some, including police officers, thought Herbert Baker was
obsessed and abnormal.

Who was Herbert Charles Baker? Hyde Heath residents
knew virtually nothing about him other than his wife had
been an invalid for years and he pushed her around the village
in a wheelchair. The only aspect of his life that did seem to be
common knowledge was that he was a lay reader at St Andrews
church. He was a member of the congregation whose job was
to assist his personal friend Rev Francis Roberts, Vicar of Little
Missenden and Hyde Heath, and other clergy, and was authorised to conduct parts of church services that did not require a
priest or minister but he was not called to full-time ministry.

Herbert Charles Baker was born in Lee, South East London
in 1886 and was the son of Herbert Baker, a master grocer,
and his wife Janet who ran a successful grocery and spirits
emporium at 229 Lee High Road. Janet Baker, the daughter
of a farm labourer, was Scottish, from the tiny village of Little
Dunkeld in Perthshire. She was a domestic servant when she

met Herbert, six years her junior, when he was travelling round Britain buying high-class goods for his business. The couple married in Dunkeld, in 1880, shortly before returning to their home in Lee. Lee was a prosperous area to live in and attracted wealthy London merchants, civil servants and professional men. Trams started operating in 1907 and houses next to the main road were the most sought after. Herbert and Janet Baker lived at 129 High Road, Lee. After 1920, when a council estate was built, those who were better off moved out.

Herbert Charles was educated at Colfe's, an independent day school in London, in the Royal Borough of Greenwich. He landed a very respectable bank clerk's job with Grindley and Co. Bank in Bishopsgate, when the City of London was bustling with activity. Bishopsgate, where trams rattled down the middle of the wide road, was close to Petticoat Lane and opposite Liverpool Street station. It was a time when the banks employed staff from their cradle to the grave. In 1912, Herbert Charles aged 26 married Ruby Crossman, 24, at the United Methodist church in Lee. In 1915, his father aged 65 died leaving £4,030, a considerable fortune then, to be administered by his wife Janet and son Herbert Charles who was one of six children. Janet Baker died in 1936. I did try to find details of her will, but despite exhaustive searches made by HM Courts and Tribunals Service, they were not able to find any record of the estate.

In the early 1920s Herbert and Ruby Baker left the bustle of Lee, with its crowds and trolley buses. They moved to the tiny, quieter and cleaner world of Hyde Heath north west of Amersham, where village folk lived off the land and there was no electricity. There was a memorial hall in the village erected in memory of fallen soldiers in the First World War, and ducks and chickens pecked their way around smallholdings.

Electricity in private village residences was still rare. It must have seemed primitive compared to Lee. In 1929 there had even been a row in Hyde Heath, reported in *The Times*, when villagers objected to new electricity poles being brought in carrying 'the electric', which would desecrate their village. That year there were only five cars in the village – one belonged to Herbert Baker. If you owned a car you were a cut above the rest. Rosemead, a small bungalow on a large plot of land just out of the centre of the village, was built in the 1920s and purchased by Herbert Baker when it was new. Before mains drainage came to the village properties had septic tanks in the garden that had to be emptied by sewerage lorries. Rosemead had an early version of a septic tank called a soakaway, which did not need to be emptied. The brick-built hole, thirty feet deep on the right-hand side of the garden drained out over a period of time.

During the Second World War, the memorial hall became a temporary HQ for civilian administration. The Home Guard did drill on the common armed with broomsticks, and later rifles, and the Women's Institute set up the Hyde Heath Jam and Preserves Factory at The Wick in the village, which was visited by the Queen Mother, in 1940. By the 1950s Hyde Heath was a village with medium and large houses and a council estate. Brian Shirley who grew up there said, 'It was a true functional semi-rural community but was suffering from divided class distinction lines. Everyone knew their place, knew each other, but did not necessarily mix.' The village was an example of how a remote hamlet grew into a straggling settlement of suburban character, bus links being forged from nearby railway stations. Cottages were made larger, more picturesque and more comfortable for the first wave of middle-class London commuters in search of a weekend home.

People in Hyde Heath watched Herbert Baker's comings and goings but were not on speaking terms with him. Some knew he left the village each day to go to London. A few said he dressed smartly and that he doffed his cap to those he regarded as equals and was determined to keep others in their place. One local said it was difficult to picture him, others knew the names Ruby and Herbert Baker, but did not know them to speak to. It was rare in a village for people not to know any detail about someone who had lived there for nearly half a century. Dennis Silcocks, head teacher at Hyde Heath Infant School next to St Andrews church from 1964–70, said, 'I may have nodded to him but didn't know who he was.'

Ruby Baker died on 5 February 1960 and was buried in the small lychgate cemetery, opposite the ancient St John the Baptist church in Little Missenden, a mile from Hyde Heath. Her tombstone read: 'In memory of Ruby Ellen Baker Borne to her great reward.' Herbert Baker commissioned a painted nativity mural in memory of Ruby, behind the altar in St Andrews church in Hyde Heath and donated a wooden cross for the top of the building.

If a kind lady doctor had been attending a patient who died, it wasn't uncommon for the husband to take a shine to her. Because Helen Davidson was unmarried there was no reason for her to repel the advances of the elderly Herbert Baker. People may have thought that as she'd been in the house regularly, there was an affair going on all the time Ruby Baker was alive. Affairs were especially frowned on in those days. But Helen Davidson lived in a different world. She did not care about having a man in her life. Not until the car crash. That changed everything. Herbert Baker persuaded this not-the-marrying-type lady to marry him. Helen was thrown into the world of marriage to a man nearly thirty years her senior.

The well-loved doctor had been involved in a serious road
traffic accident in June 1961. Two young motorcyclists lay in
hospital badly injured, one was unconscious. Helen Davidson,
a partner in the medical practice in Amersham, had caused
their multiple injuries. What a scandal that could have been
– to suspect the doctor of any wrongdoing would be unthink-
able. But the local newspapers, with the exception of a few
lines in the *Bucks Free Press*, had not reported it. Dr Davidson
was a woman who used her connections to save face. She was
a woman with power. It provides an intriguing contrast to the
woman looked up to as if she were a god, like most of the
medical profession were regarded then. Were the car crash and
the murder of the doctor part of the same story? What drove
Herbert Baker's impulse to ensnare Helen Davidson? Was the
marriage part of a carefully laid plan: a marriage of convenience to protect the doctor? It was a curious coincidence that
the announcement of her forthcoming marriage to Herbert
Baker appeared in *The Times* immediately after the motorcyclist had regained consciousness following his four-week long
coma in High Wycombe general hospital.

Many, including some close medical colleagues, didn't
realise then that Helen Davidson had married. The couple
quietly slipped away to Wimbledon, where their marriage
took place at St Mary's Parish church on 22 September 1961.
Both gave their ages as 'Of full age' almost as if they had something to hide. Herbert Baker gave his address as 26 Bishopsgate,
London EC2, which was the address of the National and
Overseas Bank, formerly Grindley and Co. Bank, from which
he had retired in 1954. Often people who didn't want anyone
to know where they lived would give their bank as an address.
Both witnesses to the ceremony were Herbert's relations. As
they emerged from the church, the couple standing side by

side in the black-and-white photograph looked more like an elderly father and daughter than husband and wife. Mrs Ann Smith, a long-standing patient of Dr Davidson and wife of a foreign diplomat said: 'Herbert Baker was a most unattractive man. He was not a catch. He did the catching.'

David Oxley, whose father was fostered by Gran Eldridge in Hyde Heath, said:

> I understood this old man was quite well off. It was certainly said much later around the villages that Dr Davidson had married a wealthy old boy. But in those days it was all relative. What would have been wealthy then would just be fairly well off now. He was wealthy enough to employ a housekeeper but you didn't have to be wealthy to do that. For ordinary working people struggling to get enough to eat, people with a moderate standard of living, were considered wealthy. I certainly wouldn't have classed Herbert Baker as wealthy living in that bungalow. I'm sure the doctor wasn't the sort of lady who would have married for money. Nobody seemed to know who he was or even bothered to know who he was.

I remember local magistrate Pam Appleby saying Dr Davidson had changed, blaming the change on her disastrous marriage. She said 'the light went out of her eyes and she no longer smiled', and that rumours were rife in Amersham society circles that Herbert Baker had persisted in a relationship with Kathleen Cook in Hyde Heath. Local people of good standing knew he spent much of his time back with her at Rosemead throughout his five-year marriage to Helen. Were the police aware of this liaison?

It was still a time when most wives were expected to put their husbands before their professions. Helen Davidson did not. Her job was her life. But on 21 January 1964 she wrote her will leaving various small legacies to her goddaughters, a nephew and a niece. She made Herbert Baker her main beneficiary. On her death, her estate was valued at £24,000. Herbert Baker had a great deal to gain from his wife's death: another house to add to his property and land portfolio. Kathleen would keep Rosemead. Very few knew the truth. Did the police dare to ask this gentleman about his wife's will and her beneficiaries? When Baker wrote his new will on 25 July 1970, he left the freehold of Rosemead to Kathleen. He also left Ashlyn to be shared between Kathleen and his nephew. Following Baker's death in 1975 his entire estate was valued at £31,000, Ashlyn then having a market value of approximately £28,000. Baker's own property, Rosemead in Hyde Heath, in its rundown state, was virtually worthless. What had happened to his personal wealth? Was this man really a 'wealthy old boy' when he married Helen Davidson in 1961? The police in 1966 were looking for a motive for Helen's murder. As they said, she was not robbed during the attack, but Herbert Baker and Kathleen Cook, who was no friend of the doctor, both stood to gain financially from her death. Money is a motive for murder.

Dr David Howell, Helen's general practice partner, who met Herbert Baker once at a sherry party one Christmas said, 'I think for some time the husband was thought to be guilty.' Det Sgt Tony Dale said:

> Baker was pulled in early for questioning and thoroughly checked out as a matter of course. He would have made a statement, which will be in the murder file at Aylesbury. There would have been a lot of detail in it. He was grilled inside and out. You always start with the person who is

closest. He was totally and utterly ruled out. He could not be implicated. He was certainly alibi'd.

The police made the mistake though of taking Herbert Baker's testimony at face value. They did not thoroughly check his version of events on 9 November 1966. He told the *Evening News* and the *Buckinghamshire Advertiser* that he and his wife spent the morning gardening together. That was curious. He failed to report his wife's actual movements: that she drove over to Hyde Heath that morning where she made a house call to Mrs Swains and her newborn twin girls in Meadow Way. Was it a lapse of memory, an oversight? Or by intention? How reliable, generally, was the 79-year-old Herbert Baker's recollections of the day's events? I wonder why the police, trained experts with the means for detection at their fingertips, did not double check Baker's statement of events that morning. Had they trodden too carefully when dealing with such a respectable gentleman? Had they believed all they were told?

It seems odd that a team of police officers had taken statements from 2,000 males around Amersham, came to Hyde Heath, dug up Kathleen Cook's garden in their search for the murder weapon but did not apparently check the sewerage soakaway, and did not make adequate house-to-house enquiries. It would have seemed natural for the police to investigate the small village properly, but it only appeared to have been done in a cursory way. The police had no knowledge to this day of Dr Davidson's home visit to Mrs Swains. If they had interviewed Derek Swains, as I did, they would have discovered a flaw in Herbert Baker's story about his wife's last movements on 9 November. They missed an opportunity. It could have thrown Baker's supposedly genuine testimony into question. Was it old age that caused him to overlook his wife's visit to Hyde Heath that morning? Or was he for some reason lying about her last movements? Swains was not the only resident to tell me the police did not come knocking at their doors. No one I spoke to in the village remembers the police calling there after the murder. Michael Baughan, who lived at Hawthorns three doors from Kathleen Cook, also confirmed 'the police never showed any interest, we were never questioned, there was no contact with the police whatsoever'. Had they called at Baughan's home they would have discovered another side to Herbert Baker. Baughan still remembers Baker's vicious temper fifty years on and being chastised by the religious fanatic one Sunday morning for rotovating his garden on the Sabbath.

It was very unusual for a woman with no enemies, a respected family doctor, a devout Christian, to be found battered to death in woodland. But Baker told the press and police, 'My wife did not have an enemy in the world. Any suggestion that any animosity was involved is way off the beam. This is the work of some poor demented soul who needs our help and our prayers.' Bereaved relatives of murder victims generally do assume there could be no motive for a loved one's murder. Det Ch Supt Williams said, 'Whoever killed Dr Davidson did so on impulse. I can't imagine that this was the result of a vendetta.' From my investigations it seems Helen Davidson did have enemies. Baker lied when he said 'My wife did not have an enemy in the world'. He kept silent about his wife's road traffic accident.

On the afternoon of 9 November Herbert Baker left home at 1.35 p.m. to go to his part-time clerical job in Chesham, which he did just to keep himself busy on the one day in the week his wife was at home. He was almost 80 years old, having retired in 1954 from Grindley and Co. Bank. He had arranged with his wife to meet some friends that evening for dinner. When he arrived home at 5.30 p.m., Helen was not there. She hadn't returned from her walk with the dog. Some hours later after his wife failed to return, and having searched for her with friends, Baker finally contacted the police. Why did he wait? Was she in the habit of coming home late? According to the *Bucks Examiner* and *Bucks Free Press*, the search for the doctor was launched at 2 a.m. the following morning. Surely Baker's reluctance to call the police immediately could be interpreted as odd. Was this the action of a man desperate to find his wife? In effect, the search and discovery of the body was delayed.

The Evening News had a photograph of Herbert Baker's face being lovingly licked by Helen Davidson's dog. The police knew that Fancy was ferocious though, and appealed for anyone who had been bitten by a dog to come forward. Det Ch Supt Williams said 'We have checked with doctors and hospitals. But it is probable that if the dog did bite the killer, he treated it himself or perhaps went to a chemist. But a dog bite could be difficult to hide and someone may have noticed.' The police still didn't get it: the alternative was that the killer was someone known and trusted by the doctor's dog. They should have been questioning anyone known to have felt confident with Fancy. Only three people could handle Helen Davidson's unsociable dog: Helen Davidson, Herbert Baker and Kathleen Cook.

'Miss Cook had a presence in the house next door after Dr Davidson's death,' said Catherine Morton, who lived with her parents in Grangehurst the house adjoining Ashlyn, Dr Davidson's home in Chesham Bois:

I wouldn't have known if she was or was not staying the night. I also wouldn't know the extent to which either

she or Mr Baker split their week between Ashlyn and
Rosemead. All I can say is that I was driven to church in
Hyde Heath on Sundays with Mr Baker and Miss Cook,
and was in the choir with Miss Cook. Mr Baker told me
he'd written a book, a mystery, and had tried to get it published.

It was 19 November 1966, ten days since the murder,
and Brig John Cheney, the retiring Chief Constable of
Buckinghamshire and old friend of Dr Davidson, demanded
the resumption of the death penalty. *The Times* reported:

> Bring back hanging, police chief urges. Brigadier John
> Cheney, who retired on Monday as Chief Constable of
> Buckinghamshire, said today, 'If the Home Secretary had
> seen what I and other police officers witnessed I am sure he
> would change his mind about hanging.' Brigadier Cheney
> was referring to the murder of Dr Helen Davidson of
> Chesham Bois whose body was found nine days ago in a
> wood off the Amersham-Beaconsfield road.

Capital punishment had ceased in Britain in 1964 and was
abolished in 1965 for a trial period. It was never reinstated.

10

Injured Parties: 1961–62

Born in 1897, Brigadier John Norman Cheney was educated at Eton College and the Royal Military Academy, Sandhurst before being commissioned in the King's Royal Rifle Corps in 1917. During a distinguished army career he served on the Western Front during the First World War and won the Croix de Guerre with Palm and was twice mentioned in dispatches. In 1946 he became Chief Constable of the East Riding of Yorkshire and, in 1953, was appointed Chief Constable of Buckinghamshire. He was an officer in Her Majesty's Bodyguard of the Honourable Corps of Gentlemen at Arms and, on ceremonial occasions, was responsible for the safety of HM the Queen. He was quoted in *The Times* as saying he was a firm believer in sponsoring good relations between police and the public and 'without goodwill and co-operation police work is made immeasurably more difficult'.

One remark I found in a biography about Brig Cheney in the *Bucks Examiner* was odd. It read: 'But the fondest memory for many people will be of the time he prosecuted himself for careless driving after being involved in an accident.' I didn't understand it. After a lot of investigation I eventually found details of an accident that occurred in 1956 in the village of Great Missenden, six miles north west of Amersham, between Brig Cheney and a 17-year-old motorcyclist called Anthony Garrett who lived on a council estate in the village. I also discovered that at that time, before the introduction of the Crime Prosecution Service, the police not only investigated the cases but the prosecution was also entirely in their hands. After the court case against Cheney for driving a motor car without reasonable consideration for other road users, for which he had pleaded guilty and subsequently received a £5 fine and his licence endorsed, articles published in *The Times* and the *Bucks Free Press* made interesting reading.

According to reports published on 2 January 1956 at about 6 p.m., as the Chief Constable was turning right, a learner motorcyclist approaching the car slowed down and turned across in front of the car. The motorcyclist mounted a pavement and came off. There was no impact between the car and the motorcycle. The motorcyclist had said his speed was not more than 20–30mph at the time, and the car was well over on his (the motorcyclist's) side of the road. The Chief Constable's defence strangely said, 'His client came to the conclusion that if he had not been there and placed his car in that position in relation to the oncoming motorcyclist, the motorcyclist would not have been placed in a dilemma, and the accident, whatever the cause, would not have happened.' I had the impression that the confrontation was being played down by the press. Brig Cheney's actions immediately after the incident were certainly not honourable. He did not immediately stop his car at the scene. Instead he continued driving along the road as if he thought he could get away with it, until, according to the *Bucks Free Press* 'a woman shouted to him that there had been an accident. He then saw the motorcyclist lying on the ground and went to his assistance.'

There may have been 'no impact between the car and the motorcycle' but I learnt from Mr Garrett's widow, Felicity, that the incident had left Anthony, who was then an apprentice toolmaker, in hospital with a broken pelvis, multiple injuries to his lower body, traumatised and off work for six months. Felicity met Anthony a year after the accident and they married in 1961. She said:

> Even though Brig Cheney was fined there was more to the crash. When it happened Cheney was on the wrong side of the road on a blind corner, and Anthony who was coming in the opposite direction, could not take avoiding action because there was nowhere for him to go. The motorbike went up a No Waiting sign on the roadside, Anthony was thrown off and the bike came down on top of him and crushed him. His family was disgusted with Brig Cheney who did not contact them once to find out how Anthony was. He suffered terrible headaches for much of his life and always said they were caused by the accident. He was discharged from the army on medical grounds.

In the 1960s, Brig Cheney lived in Hill House, Chalk Lane in Hyde Heath, about half a mile from the centre of the village. It was an impressive 1930s double-fronted house, set in half an acre of grounds well back from the road with a big in-and-out gravel driveway. On the opposite side of the road was a small meadow with a mound, the site of a Norman keep and bailey castle dating back to 1086. The Rev Francis Roberts and his wife were neighbours close-by at the Old Vicarage, at the end of Chalk Lane.

Brian Shirley was a newspaper delivery boy in Hyde Heath in the early 1960s and later became a serving police cadet at police headquarters in Aylesbury. His mother was the daily help at Hill House:

> It was a bit of a status symbol to have a daily. I never went inside, that was my mother's department. She cleaned there two mornings a week for two hours. The money was useful. In the 1960s tradesmen were only allowed to go to the rear entrance of houses. I cut the lawns during the summer school holidays to earn additional pocket money. Brig Cheney was a real policeman's policeman ... officer and a true gentleman.

About a year after starting my research for this book, I drove to Bletchingley in Surrey to give my talk about Ruth Ellis to the Women's Institute. That day remains clear in my mind. I arrived early at the village hall. Their president, Carol Bain, greeted me. We chatted. She casually asked what story I was currently working on. I told her about the murder of Dr Davidson in 1966 in Amersham. She told me how she grew up in Amersham and recounted the story of a motor-cyclist who had been involved in a road traffic accident with the doctor sometime in the 1960s. She could not remember the year it happened. 'His name was Michael Larcombe,' she said. 'We went to school together, Challoner's Grammar school in Amersham which was co-educational. He was in my class.' I couldn't believe it. After months of searching for an unknown motorcyclist, by sheer coincidence, a total stranger confirmed his identity:

He was a very good-looking boy, had beautiful dark, wavy hair and was always after the girls, flirted all the time. To get into Challoner's he was obviously a bright boy but he was lazy. You got the impression he just wanted to get out whereas other boys wanted to stay on. There was concern the doctor was going to be charged. She must have felt terrible especially in her profession and in her standing in the community. People wondered if she was tired that day, working all hours tending to patients, and not concentrating on her driving. Rumours were that Michael Larcombe wasn't the same again after the crash, he became withdrawn and there was great speculation Michael was involved with the doctor's murder.

After this chance meeting with Carol Bain, virtually no one I spoke to knew anything, or admitted to knowing anything, about the serious road traffic accident involving Dr Davidson. After all, she had treated the sick in Amersham for twenty-one years, had 3,500 patients on her register and was a pillar of the community. Apart from a few vague recollections of a 'not very serious' accident, and one person thinking she'd read of a motorcyclist being killed, it was as if it had never happened.

Det Sgt Tony Dale had mentioned a road traffic accident involving the doctor and a motorcyclist whose name he couldn't remember:

In about 1965 she [Dr Davidson] was coming down Station Road in Amersham and pulling out to turn right into First Avenue. Coming down was an 18-year-old on a motor-bike. She cut across his path. He hit her. She was reported for careless driving. I don't think he was badly injured. His name would be in the murder file at Aylesbury. I wouldn't

have thought it was as far back as '63. The press would have
been told about it during the daily briefings. It probably
made a snippet in the papers at the time. The press used
to come in to the police station and were allowed to read
the Incident and Accident Books. That's how it was in
those days.

It was an enormous task combing through years of
Buckinghamshire newspapers at the Newspaper Library
in North London. Dale said the accident occurred around
1965. Nothing really useful turned up. But I was struck by
the high number of road traffic accidents, bumps, scrapes,
serious injuries and deaths reported every week in the 1960s
in all the local papers and described as 'carnage on the roads'.
Ch Con Brig Cheney, in his 1960 New Year message to the
Buckinghamshire press, appealed for better driving standards in the county, to 'Stop the Horror … and Make 1960 a
Safer Place on the Roads'. What a wonderful irony – it was
exactly four years since his mishap in Great Missenden made
banner headlines. One name that regularly cropped up in the
Buckinghamshire papers in the late 1950s and early '60s was
Lady Violet Attlee. She lived in Great Missenden with her
husband Clement Attlee, the former British prime minister,
who oversaw the introduction of the National Health Service
in 1948. Lady Violet was a notoriously bad driver and had
been involved in a string of reported road traffic accidents, one
included a fatality. She escaped prosecution on every occasion.
National road safety campaigner, Lt Comdr William Boaks
Retd, an eccentric who had styled himself as the minister of
road safety and was tolerated by the police and legal profession, had an obsession against drivers with poor driving skills.
He claimed Lady Attlee had been protected from criminal

proceedings because she was the wife of the former prime minister. The Attlee family were neighbours of the Davidson family in Portinscale Road, in Putney, when Helen Davidson was growing up.

I finally found the report I'd been searching for. It was on the front page of the *Bucks Free Press* dated 7 July 1961, tucked in a left-hand column amongst thirty or so other articles on the page. Immediately I became aware of inconsistencies. Beneath the heading 'Two Hurt in Road Crash', it read:

> Two young motorcyclists were seriously injured when they were involved in a collision with a car at the Station Road junction at Amersham on Friday. One of the motor-cyclists, Michael Larcombe, an 18-year-old learner driver, of 'Copperkins', Copperkins Lane, Amersham sustained severe head injuries. The other, Brian Woolsey, a 21-year-old student who gave his address as the Roman Catholic Church, Amersham Road, Chesham Bois, fractured his left leg and foot. The younger driver was taken to Amersham hospital but was later transferred to High Wycombe hospital where both were detained. The car was driven by Dr Helen Davidson of 'Ashlyn' North Road, Chesham Bois. On Wednesday a spokesman for the hospital said that Larcombe, who sustained fractures of the skull and was still uncon-scious, was showing slight improvement and that Woolsey was comfortable.

The newspaper incorrectly reported that Michael Larcombe was 18. He was actually 21.

It was not what I expected. I later wrote to Tony Dale saying two motorcyclists were involved in the crash, not one. He was surprised. In his reply he wrote: 'I have no recollection of *two* motorcyclists being involved in the accident. That's totally new to me.' In fairness Dale was not promoted to Amersham CID until 1962. He had joined Buckinghamshire Constabulary in 1955, and in 1958, aged 23, was given his own beat for three years at Little Chalfont, a village two and a half miles east of Amersham. He probably would not have been aware of all the happenings at Amersham police station, which at that time was a forty-foot-long weather-boarded hut built at the rear of a brick council house in the old town. Ch Con Brig Cheney described it in a report to *The Times* as the 'Black Hole of Calcutta', the worst police station in England. Presumably an accurate police report about the two motorcyclists was entered in the police station's Accident Book, which was for brief records of accidents reported or attended by the police. It gave details of motorists involved, location, whether there were injuries or damage only to vehicles and was meant as a quick reference for the police if there was a query.

There were no further details about the car crash in the *Bucks Free Press* the following week, and not a word in any other local papers, despite the story having all the right ingredients: a well-loved local doctor, a pillar of the community, a good-looking motorcyclist lying unconscious in hospital, almost as if there had been a news blackout. Was pressure applied to suppress the incident thereby avoiding a scandal? Now was the time to really start 'digging'. With an extraordinary amount of luck I traced Michael Larcombe, who was the one solid link with another side of Dr Davidson. Now in his seventies, Michael lives quietly in Essex.

It was Friday 30 June 1961, the end of the first week of the Wimbledon tennis championships in London which was celebrating its 75th anniversary, the BBC TV broadcast was due to begin at 1.35 p.m., and temperatures over the entire country had soared to 85°F. Michael Larcombe had finished his lunch in the work's canteen at Brazil's meat-processing factory in Old Amersham where he was employed as an industrial baker, then drove home on his motorbike to Chesham Bois, where he rented a first-floor flat in a large detached house called Copperkins in Copperkins Lane. He was proud of his steady job where he'd worked for three years despite jibes from his father Charlie Larcombe that he 'just made steak and kidney pies for a living'. Michael had not long turned 21 and with his thick, slicked back hair, blue eyes and full mouth he looked like a film star. He wore the essential black leather jacket and drove a top of the range German motorbike, had a steady girlfriend and loved life. Quite by chance, when he reached Top Amersham that lunchtime he met his good chum Brian Woolsey, also aged 21. Brian was an artist and potter, known as Bru, his uncle was a Roman Catholic priest at Our Lady of Perpetual Succour church in Chesham Bois. The young men had known each other for four months and shared a passion for motorbikes. They said 'Hi', revved their engines and headed south together along Station Road, riding side by side towards Amersham. 'We went under the railway bridge. There was a long, fast downhill section of the road, for about one and a half miles. We were just enjoying the hot sun on our backs.' Michael never dreamt that when he popped home that day his life would change forever in a split second. There was a screech of tyres as the motorcyclists approached a turning on the left into First Avenue, then an almighty thud. Dr Davidson was driving her car in the opposite direction up Station Road. She turned right into First Avenue, cut across the path of the young motorcyclists, her car juddered across in front of them and stopped.

Trevor Richardson, who lived with his family at Pink House on the corner of Hill Avenue at its junction with Station Road, said there had been five or six accidents there over the years:

> We often heard dull thuds, metal hitting metal. Dad always made absolutely sure that the road was clear before turning in to the house. It was a dangerous little corner. Our lounge faced the road. That day we heard a thud and a bit of a screech. I remember a guy lying in the middle of the road. He was wearing dark clothes, the motorcycle was dark and it had skidded up towards the house. Mum and Dad went out to help. I was told to stay at the gate. All the neighbours were on the scene as fast as us. Mum came back and said it was Dr Davidson. She was an important person to us as our family doctor. We were so pleased she wasn't hurt. It was a big thing for us. It's not every day your doctor is involved in a crash outside your house. The car was left in the middle of the road.

Michael Larcombe was not the same after the accident. The brain damage he sustained that day began 'an unstoppable sex change'. He suffered a fractured skull, fifteen fractures to his face, which required a facial rebuild, lost seven teeth, a fractured femur and dislocated hip, and paralysis. The medical profession, as was the case then, was indifferent to Michael's new personality problem. There was no counselling, it was just a case of living or dying. Michael said, 'All I could do was make noises to the police officer who came once to High Wycombe general hospital to take my statement, only just managing to write replies on a notepad.' Michael would never forgive Dr Davidson. His brother David said:

When you look back he was a Jack the Lad, a ladies' man, he used to enjoy life to the full but the accident rearranged his life when he started thinking he was a woman. It was awful to see. He had totally changed. The difference the accident made to him was beyond anything you could comprehend. Doctors started putting drugs into his food in hospital, hormones, androgens, to keep him as a man. When I look back, how his life has been, I wouldn't have wanted it. I suppose he accepts it. How he is and how it happened has always hurt me. Father couldn't accept it. In those days being effeminate was a taboo subject. All this only nine months after his twenty-first birthday. Over the years he's swung from male to female.

Tony Dale was specific when it came to details of how the Chief Constable, Brig John Cheney, leapt to Helen Davidson's defence and became personally involved in the incident. He said:

The two knew each other and went to the same church in Hyde Heath. She'd been reported for careless driving. The Chief put the case out to a private solicitor who was not in the Force area to make an impartial decision. Because he knew her he didn't think he should make a decision. He didn't want any repercussions later, so the names were changed. There was no suggestion in the letter that Cheney knew the woman. It was a fair way of determining a possible successful prosecution. The Chief was falling over himself not to be accused of sweeping it under the carpet. That was the whole purpose of him sending it away. The Chief asked the solicitors: 'Would you prosecute?' The answer came back: 'No'. Cheney went along with the solicitor's recommendation. The case didn't come to anything. The bloke

started going mentally funny a year or so later. He accused
the police of a cover up.

I asked if it was usual procedure for the Chief Constable to
send a case to a solicitor for an opinion rather than let a court
decide like anyone else. 'It was rare. It was absolutely proper',
said Dale. I asked if he could think of any other occasion when
Brig Cheney wrote to a private solicitor asking for independent advice about a case. Dale said 'I had no knowledge of
any other occasions. It was unusual for him to take something
like this so seriously.'

To me it seemed odd that Brig Cheney, the head of the
Buckinghamshire police force, should take a personal interest
and become involved in an alleged minor road traffic accident
that had attracted virtually no interest from the press. The
motorcyclist was 'just a petty criminal' according to Dale.
Something was not right. Cheney's unusual action seemed a
neat way of alerting a solicitor to a potentially awkward investigation that could harm Amersham's hierarchy.

There was a world of difference between Michael
Larcombe's humble background and Helen Davidson who
was a public figure moving in high circles. He was born on
14 October 1939 and was brought up on a sprawling council
estate in Milton Road, Chesham renowned for its high levels
of crime. His parents Charlie and Gladys Larcombe had rented
their council house since 1936. Charlie served most of the
Second World War as a private in the RAMC (Royal Army
Medical Corps) in Algiers. He didn't see his son again until the
end of the war in 1945. Like many returning service personnel
Charlie had changed. He was unsure of his former skills and
uncertain of being with other people. Michael had a weak
constitution as a result of contracting whooping cough as a

young child and spent much of his childhood in and out of
Harefield Hospital undergoing lung surgery. Against the odds,
at the age of 11 he was strong enough to go back to White
Hills primary school in Chesham and sit the 11+ examinations,
which he passed. Charlie Larcombe, who didn't see education as worthwhile, felt no pride when his son gained a place
at Challoner's co-educational grammar school in Amersham.
He told his son 'Don't get any ideas of staying on'. Despite
disfiguring scars from double lung surgery, Michael belonged
to the boxing club and was never beaten in the ring. In 1953
he won the interschool championship against the boys from
the local secondary modern school. He left school at 15 on
the orders of his father; Charlie Larcombe was not prepared to
keep him at home. 'He was a hard socialist,' said Michael. 'Dad
said, "You're not going to university". That's the man he was.
It wasn't financial. It was just him. He was anxious to see me
earning.'

In 1954 Michael was accepted as a trade apprentice at the
De Haviland Aeronautical Technical School in Portsmouth. At
the end of the third year he returned home to his parents'
house, unemployed. 'Dad had had enough and told me I could
get out as soon as I liked,' said Michael:

I saw an advertisement in the local paper for a flat and
went to see Margo Morris in her antique shop opposite
Amersham station. She approved of me and I got the flat
in her house Copperkins in Copperkins Lane in Chesham
Bois. I'd gone from a notorious council estate to this beautiful detached house full up with paintings and antique
furniture. It was a time of great happiness. I had very little
money, was out of work again and had to find a job. I went
to Brazil's. The manager said I could work in the bake house

where they produced meat pies. We never went hungry.
At 9 a.m., the pies would start running down a conveyor
belt. Everyone nicked them but Brazil's were very good to
employees. At lunchtime we had free meals.

On 1 August 1961, exactly one month after the road traffic
accident, the day Michael Larcombe regained consciousness in
High Wycombe hospital, Helen Davidson and Herbert Baker
announced their forthcoming marriage. Why would Helen
suddenly forfeit her privacy for an elderly man whom she did
not love, a man used to being looked after by his housekeeper
Kathleen Cook? How much had the accident affected her? Did
she feel guilty for what had happened? Was she concerned for
her personal safety? As well as a GP, she was a police doctor who
served on a panel of local GPs to be called on in cases such as
rape and domestic violence. Did she feel vulnerable? In a small
town like Amersham, the downside of being a police doctor was
that villains in the town would soon know of her predicament.
    Michael Larcombe said:

> The police who were in close contact with my father,
> visiting him several times at the furniture department in
> the Co-op in Chesham where he worked, said they had all
> the evidence they needed to bring a conviction against the
> doctor … the position of the car on the road etc. They said
> it didn't matter that I couldn't remember what happened in
> the crash.

The petty sessions hearing was set for 15 February 1962. This
court, now known as the magistrates' court, dealt with the
more minor criminal cases that threatened to overwhelm the
quarter sessions. The moment Helen Davidson stepped into

the courtroom she was home and dry. She had the best legal advice from Allan Janes, a leading firm of solicitors in High Wycombe that had enjoyed a good reputation since its formation in 1931, as well as Capt John Allen, an expert witness and advisor to the Ministry of Transport on road accidents. The prosecution, as was customary then, was in the hands of the police. It was an extraordinary fact that Brig Cheney, the Chief Constable of Buckinghamshire, was in a position to personally prosecute his close friend Helen Davidson in the case brought against her for careless driving.

Later in 1962, a Royal Commission on the police said that it was not acceptable for the police to use the same officers to investigate and prosecute cases, recommending that all police forces should have their own prosecuting solicitors departments. Some forces did set up their own prosecuting solicitors departments, others continued to use local firms of solicitors for advice on prosecutions but did not have to act on their advice. The Crime Prosecution Service was not set up until 1986.

Michael Larcombe and Brian Woolsey had to rely on assurances from the local police that Dr Davidson would be properly questioned by the prosecution. 'I've a strong picture of me in court,' said Michael:

In the public section were reporters and members of the public. One of the magistrates on the Bench read out the charge of careless driving against Dr Davidson. I testified as a prosecution witness. I was very ill but the impression the court gave of my condition was the opposite. They talked of a 'complete recovery' and so on. When I took the stand I took the oath. Brig Cheney who was in full uniform asked me what I remembered of the crash. All I could say was that I couldn't remember anything. Once they heard that they

dispensed with me and all the action was against Brian. He
looked perfectly normal but had a bad limp. He was the key
witness and took the oath. He knew what happened. They
tore into him with technical jargon … it left you bewildered.
Statements like: 'Were you six feet from the kerb … in the
middle of the road?' It was the doctor's word against his.
Brian could only answer the questions put to him, nothing
else. Before the case the police told my father they had all the
evidence they needed for a prosecution. Cheney withheld all
the evidence. He didn't ask the right questions. Dr Davidson
omitted all the factual detail. She was as guilty as sin. When he
questioned her she said she drove up Station Road and it was
all clear except for a lorry much further up the road, and two
motorbikes went into her. And when Cheney questioned the
police officers who took the stand he didn't ask any relevant
questions. There was a cover-up, a stain on everyone in the
police force because of what happened in court. The doctor
had been charged with careless driving but her friend Brig
Cheney prosecuted her. They connived and schemed and had
it all set up. When they announced the case was dismissed
because of insufficient evidence Brian was particularly per-
turbed. He stood up and said to the judge: 'Your honour.
Your honour. That's not how the accident happened.' The
impression given to the court was that we were speeding.
Brian knew our story had been distorted. I knew we were
not racing. A lorry was coming up the hill towards us. Dr
Davidson was in her car directly behind the lorry. She had
no vision of what was coming from the opposite direction.
She turned straight across in front of us. She didn't see us.

In Michael's eyes Brig Cheney had used his power, influence and gone to considerable lengths to obstruct the course

of justice and had no intention of seeing his friend Helen Davidson sent to trial for a careless driving offence. The assurance that had been given to Charlie Larcombe by the police that they had all the necessary evidence for a conviction came to nothing. Michael said:

> Afterwards the police were very sincere. They said they were terribly sorry to my father, that they had all the evidence when they went into the witness box but the prosecuting counsel, Brig Cheney, didn't ask the relevant questions. That meant Dr Davidson in turn didn't have to explain things properly, and looked innocent.

Unknown of course to Michael's father, Charlie Larcombe, Brig Cheney had already been advised by an independent solicitor before the case came to court, not to prosecute. By inadequately questioning the defendant Helen Davidson, Cheney did not fulfil his role as prosecutor. He had followed the solicitor's advice. If Michael Larcombe and Brian Woolsey had been properly advised they could have brought a civil prosecution against Dr Davidson. But they were in no position to do so through ignorance and financial constraints.

If a respected GP were to be found guilty of dangerous driving, and having also caused multiple injuries, it would have been a blot on her career, a serious threat to the credibility of her medical practice in Amersham, and on the medical profession as a whole. In court she received all the help she needed: a first-class solicitor for her defence, a road traffic accident specialist, and her friend Brig Cheney, the Chief Constable of Buckinghamshire, who acted for the prosecution but did not do his job. In effect the case was thrown. Helen Davidson, like Lady Violet Attlee, it seems, was immune to prosecution.

The article about the dangerous driving charge brought against the doctor, published in the *Bucks Free Press*, was headlined: 'MOTOR-CYCLISTS SAID TO BE RACING BEFORE AMERSHAM CRASH, Careless Driving Charge Against Doctor Dismissed.' It was lengthy in comparison to the brief description of the crash in the same paper the previous year. It took up a third of a page in the 16 February 1967 edition. Both Mr Allan Janes and Capt John Allen who defended Helen Davidson in court, were quoted in the article. But something was missing. It was curious that Brig Cheney's name for the prosecution did not appear once; he was after all the Chief Constable. The doctor's role in the accident was smoothed over. It was written up in vague terms giving the impression she was innocent of any wrongdoing – the opposite of the two motorcyclists' involvement who were accused of racing each other down Station Road. It was this state of affairs that subsequently created Larcombe's deep resentment for the doctor.

Fifty years later he still holds her responsible for wrecking his life. At the time, he was spurred on by his desire for revenge for the accident he said she had caused. He said, 'Nobody came to the front door when I called at her house. I can't say what would have happened in the heat of the moment if she had been in.' The car crash and the outcome of the court hearing had given him enough reason to take revenge. In his eyes she had failed him; she was protected by the power of people with influence. All Michael cared about was that Dr Davidson should have accepted responsibility for the crash and admitted she was in the wrong. In his eyes justice had not been done. He had been maimed for life.

Was Dr Davidson murdered then because of her role in the car crash in 1961?

II

Countdown: 1962–66

On 27 April 1962, two months after the court case in which his friend Helen Davidson had been cleared of the careless driving charge, Ch Con Brig Cheney announced to *The Times* that the Buckinghamshire police were reviving the Courtesy Cop idea that had been tried out in Lancashire before the Second World War. The campaign to advise rather than prosecute would be directed to all road users and tried out for two months. Cheney said: 'Anything is worth trying. The accident figures at the moment can be compared with the casualties of a minor war. I want to see the effect of concentrating police at certain times where they will attempt to educate motorists and others in accident prevention … wilful and flagrant disregard of the law would not be tolerated.'

Cheney's ideology had little effect – crime rates generally were on the increase. In 1963 the government announced it was the worst year so far this century for crimes with more homicides, theft, violence and suicides. The affluent society was being blamed as one of the main causes of Britain's rocketing post-war crime figures. It was a problematic 1963 for Buckinghamshire police. Under Ch Con Brig Cheney's watch, the Profumo Scandal, that began in the county, broke in March. John Profumo, the Secretary of State for War in the Conservative government, had become involved with 19-year-old call girl Christine Keeler two years before at a house party at Cliveden, Lord Astor's mansion eleven miles south west of Amersham. Also present at the party was society osteopath and party arranger Dr Stephen Ward, a long-standing friend of Christine. Christine was also involved with a senior Soviet naval attaché at the Soviet embassy in London. The three-way affair led to one of the greatest political scandals of the twentieth century and the downfall of the Conservative government the following year. On 8 August, the biggest ever robbery to date in British history happened at Ledburn twenty miles north of Amersham: the Great Train Robbery was committed. Thieves ambushed the Glasgow to Euston night mail train at Bridego Railway Bridge, near Ledburn. They stole £2.6 million in used bank notes. It would become known as the crime of the century and would turn out to be the biggest crime ever in the Buckinghamshire Constabulary's history. The bulk of the stolen money was never recovered. Investigators including Buckinghamshire Police, the British Transport Police and the post office were on the scene in the early hours of the morning. Det Con John Bailey, of the Photography Department of the Buckinghamshire Constabulary, was called out at 5.30 a.m. to take photographs at the scene of the crime. Three years later he would be called out to Hodgemoor Wood to photograph the scene of the crime following the murder of Helen Davidson.

Michael Larcombe was back on the Milton Road council estate and being kept by his parents. He could no longer look after himself in his flat at Copperkins in Chesham Bois. He was often bed-bound, wanted to die and overdosed on sleeping tablets a few times. Although he tried to get a job, there were long periods of unemployment because he was unemployable:

> I met a self-employed gardener through one of the social workers. He employed me. He was a good chap, late middle age and knew about my accident. We cut hedges and creosoted fences. I worked in a pub in the village of Chenies, but I was also claiming National Assistance, which was stopped because of my earnings. I was offered a position as assistant in a hardware shop in top Amersham, later at a greengrocer's where the girls could see I was wearing a bra and said they'd like to keep me as a woman. It was confusing. They knew I'd been in a crash.

Michael was in and out of St John's Hospital, which was the main psychiatric hospital for Buckinghamshire, previously known as the Stone House mental asylum. It formed the backbone of in-patient mental health care. He was looking more and more effeminate, enjoyed dressing up as a woman and went to London where he strutted around Soho in his high-heeled shoes. One emotion though was foremost in his mind: revenge. He could not escape the feeling. The dismissal of the careless driving case against Dr Davidson haunted him. As far as he was concerned, money and power, which he didn't have, bought justice. 'I'd seen the doctor's address in the local paper,' he said:

> A couple of times I went round to her home to kill her. How she could carry on driving and not get her keys thrown away beats me. She had everything: a lovely home,

a job, a husband. If only she'd acted with honour. I looked through the front window before knocking on the front door, then the back door when nobody came, to confront her. Nobody answered the door.

The window in Dr Davidson's consulting room at the medical practice in Amersham at the bottom of Gore Hill looked out across Broadway to the London Transport bus garage, with its constant hubbub of double-decker buses, Green Line coaches and local people coming and going. Built in 1936, it was the first London Transport garage to be sited prominently alongside an important main road close to a historic town centre. Next to the side entrance of the bus garage was B&M Motors, where assistants served customers with petrol from a kiosk on the forecourt. Often there would be a queue of cars waiting to be serviced at the back. From the bus garage it was a two-minute walk to Amersham police headquarters at the eastern end of Broadway. This was the black-boarded wooden shed that Brig Cheney had described in an outburst to *The Times* as the worst police station in England. It consisted of four small rooms: an inquiry office with two benches, a general office housing secretarial staff and a switchboard operator, an office for the area's CID man and a joint office for the sergeant and inspector. There were no cells, which meant that prisoners had to be taken to Chesham police station to be locked up. The lighting was poor and it was heated by three coal-burning stoves.

On 14 November 1964, the police finally vacated the simple building which had probably reflected an earlier era in policing, that of the genial, respected and authoritative police officer who knew everyone on his beat. Det Sgt Tony Dale said, 'We had a great feeling of nostalgia for the old wooden huts. At first we didn't know what to do with the space in the new place.' The police were rehoused in a modern police station located in the new civic centre in Top Amersham near the railway station. It was a new era, and the image of the police as a whole was changing. In a nationwide poll at that time, 40 per cent of people in Britain thought police took bribes, a third thought they used unfair means to get their information and a third thought they distorted evidence in court.

It was around April 1965 when Michael Larcombe learned what it was like to be victimised by the police. He could not recall the precise date but remembered it was a cold and wet spring day when there was a loud knock on the front door:

> I was living with mum and dad and they were both out at work. It was about 10 o'clock in the morning. Two plain-clothes police officers, in their thirties, came round out of the blue and said they were going to arrest me. They came straight in, said that the labour exchange in Chesham had been broken into the previous night, a lot of equipment was stolen, the place set on fire, and tried to pin it on me. They said, 'We know it was you. We're going to get you Larcombe. We have evidence to show it was you.'

Michael, now with his high-pitched, distorted voice and who enjoyed wearing women's lingerie and lipstick, was an ideal target for criticism by police officers that didn't understand effeminate men. They searched his bedroom expecting to find stolen office equipment but all they found was a suitcase under his bed containing lingerie and make-up:

> They said, 'You sissy boy. We can deal with sissy boys.' They kept on at me to admit to the arson. They handcuffed me and took me in a car to the old Chesham police station

in Broad Street, parked in the yard behind, then bundled me into a cell for half an hour. I was taken to an interview room and interviewed by two other police officers. The questioning went on till early evening. I had no solicitor, no food, no cup of tea. They kept saying 'It's easiest if you just admit it to save time and expense. You're the little sissy boy who likes wearing brassieres and knickers.' It went right over my head. I felt sorry for them. Then they told me I was free to go. The police came back to the house when mum and dad were there and told them about the suitcase of underwear which we had never talked about previously. Things were different then. They told dad they wanted to search his bedroom. He refused. He said there was nothing in there. In the end they backed down and went.

The police had it in for Michael Larcombe, as if by having no proper job and dubious sexual leanings he had been turned into a villain. Half the population then thought homosexuality disgusting. Because it was illegal, anyone at all with an unusual sexual orientation had to keep it secret and was regarded as a liar and a criminal; it was a sign of dangerous intentions. The police service then was very macho, so anyone showing effeminate tendencies would not have been accepted. One retired senior police officer said

> There were strong, bigoted feelings about 'queers', as they were commonly called in the force, particularly among lower ranking officers from working class backgrounds. Officers were inclined to bunch them altogether, child molesters, homosexuals, flashers, peepers and other sexual perverts. A lot of it was canteen talk and very few, if any, could give a decent explanation for their views.

As the summer of 1966 began, national optimism was running high. Britain in the Swinging Sixties was a country of boutiques and bistros, miniskirts, dolly birds, and lots of legs on show, and The Beatles played their last British concert at Wembley. There was Carnaby Street, photographer David Bailey and supermodel Twiggy. The economy was booming. For many it was a time of excitement, freedom and the feeling that anything goes. For millions of ordinary people the event that defined the year was the FIFA Football World Cup hosted by England. In July football fever swept the nation. England's defeat of West Germany by four goals to two, after extra time, underlined the atmosphere in the summer of 1966. There was a feeling of greatness. Bobby Moore's team were regarded as heroes, and TV commentator Kenneth Wolstenholme's 'They think it's all over … it is now' still reverberates to this day.

In the small market town of Chesham there was a spate of arson attacks. On Wednesday 6 July, the first fire severely damaged Springfield House in Springfield Road. Shortly after 9 p.m., police and fire appliances were called out as flames leapt through the roof of the large detached house which had been empty, though securely locked, for eight years. The fire started at the foot of the staircase where creosote or tar had been spread into a pool on the ground. Det Insp Ernest Lund of Amersham CID told the *Bucks Examiner* they had taken away samples of burnt wood to be examined by experts. Eighteen days later, on Sunday 24 July, four more properties in the town were set alight. Springfield House was under attack for the second time. Scrawled on one of its inside walls, using charred timber, the arsonist left an intriguing but unexplained message: 'HELP D.D.' Springfield Road was parallel to Hospital Hill and a stone's throw from Chesham Cottage Hospital with its small outpatients department and where some surgery was carried out. Coincidentally it was here that Dr Davidson attended weekly clinics and practised as an anaesthetist every Thursday and Friday.

I followed the news in local papers over three consecutive weeks about the 'fire bug', which included an artist's sketch and description of a man aged 38–48 with a round face, ruddy complexion, pointed chin, clean shaven, with a broken tooth at the front, whom the police wished to interview in connection with the fires. By the end of July, it seemed the man in the picture had given up, and in common with most arsonists, was not caught. The troubled person, probably angry at the world and wanting attention, had satisfied his desire for a thrill and the sense of power that setting fire to something gave him. People I spoke to who have lived in Chesham for many years did not seem to know anything about the arson attacks. 'People didn't take much notice of that sort of thing,' one resident said.

The arson attacks happened four months before the murder of Dr Davidson in Hodgemoor Wood, on 9 November 1966. It would seem natural to associate the works of an arsonist and the smeared message using charred wood on the wall of Springfield House, with illegally lit bonfires at Hodgemoor Wood and a length of charred timber believed to be the weapon used to kill Dr Davidson. Did the police investigate to see if the incidents were linked? Could the doctor's murder have been the work of an arsonist? Was someone crying out for help? Was the daubed creosote the work of a local gardener or maintenance person?

For Michael Larcombe there was no Football World Cup euphoria. His parents, after thirty years on the council estate in Chesham, moved that summer to a new semi-detached house in Somerset. Michael's brother David thought his parents would take Michael with them. They didn't. It was the end of May. Michael was working on the petrol pumps at B&M Motors, next to the bus garage, and found temporary lodgings with a friend's parents who lived across the road. Four weeks later he left his job abruptly:

> I felt fine but was still going round saying I would murder Dr Davidson and began to feel dreadfully ill. The family I was living with asked me to find a place of my own. I couldn't find anywhere. That's when I started sleeping rough in the workshop belonging to B&M Motors. There was nothing untoward doing that in those days. Or I'd sleep on the buses next door at Amersham bus garage. I slept upstairs on the back seat of a double decker for about five nights. When it was dark, about eleven o'clock, I went in through the main entrance of the garage. It wasn't locked. My possessions consisted of a brown holdall, some toiletries and a towel. I'd come out at about five the next morning. I knew most of the bus drivers. One started the bus up one morning with me on it. He wasn't particularly concerned. The bus drivers who knew me felt sorry for me.

The effects of the car crash five years earlier had brought Michael down to this level. He was 26 and in trouble. Early in the morning, on 24 June, he stole a service van from B&M Motors, took £95 in cash from the safe, a tank of petrol and drove the vehicle away. He said:

> I'd had enough. I picked up my bag from behind a pew in St Mary's church where I'd left it for safekeeping and drove to London where I bought an array of pretty dresses. Then I drove to Petersfield and rested in a comfortable hotel in

the town. It was the only course for me. I was desperately
ill. I had to rest or I'd have been on the street. But I said to
myself I'd have to face it.

On 30 June 1966, Michael gave himself up at Amersham police
station, returned £46 of the stolen money and was remanded
to Oxford prison. After being charged at Amersham magistrates' court, with taking and driving away the van without the
consent of the owner, using the van while uninsured, using it
without a driving licence and stealing the £95 while he was
an employee at B&M Motors, his story was reported in the
Bucks Examiner dated Friday 15 July. He had pleaded guilty to
all four charges. The court heard that he was tired, just wanted
a rest and would probably do it again. A statement he made
was read out in court. He said he'd been living rough for six
weeks, had been scrounging from friends, claiming National
Assistance, had been sleeping in vehicles at the garage. He was
described as a grammar school boy who at the age of 21 had
been involved in a serious accident for which he had been
in and out of hospital, and had received psychiatric treatment. He was remanded in custody at Winchester prison for
a psychiatric report. Michael said, 'I was in a hospital cell with
washbasin, toilet and soft bed and was treated well. It was there
I ended up in solitary confinement after being made love to
by another patient. These affairs do develop in prison. I was
not a man. I was something in between. The prison wardens
regarded me as just another sissy boy.'

On 28 July, Michael appeared again at Amersham magistrates' court for the verdict where he received a six-month
sentence and was taken to B Wing at Oxford prison to begin
his sentence. 'Most of the screws were nice but there was one
who was a bastard. He used to say "Little sissy boy, I've got a

job for you", and I was taken across the yard where I spent days peeling potatoes. The prison governor found out and said he'd try to help me. I was put back in the prison to do washing up.'

From August 1966 onwards, Buckinghamshire police dominated the front pages of the local papers. Labour's home secretary, Roy Jenkins, said Buckinghamshire and neighbouring constabularies were not up to the job of policing in the modern world and wanted amalgamation of forces. The County Police Committee opposed the government's scheme to amalgamate Buckinghamshire, Oxfordshire, Oxford City, Berkshire and Reading police forces. The *Bucks Examiner* reported that the home secretary thought the scheme was in the interest of police efficiency for the area as a whole and that the three counties had 'common crime and traffic problems which can be dealt with by the amalgamation now of the three counties so that the whole area is policed by a single force'. At the beginning of September, Buckinghamshire police who were still objecting to a voluntary amalgamation were ordered by the home secretary to amalgamate. It was the first case in which Roy Jenkins announced his intention to use his power to promote a compulsory amalgamation. Ch Con Brig John Cheney was not prepared to make any comment. A week later Brig Cheney, then aged 68, who had been Chief Constable of Buckinghamshire since 1953, announced his retirement. The *Bucks Examiner* reported that Cheney would probably be best remembered for his work when he was in charge of the Great Train Robbery investigation, and 'most fondly' for the careless driving case in which he prosecuted himself.

Thirteen years after the accident involving Cheney and the young motorcyclist Anthony Garrett who was seriously injured, the *Bucks Examiner*, with its absurdly worded report, still appeared to be sweeping Cheney's role in it under the carpet. On 7 October 1966, the *Bucks Examiner* headline read: 'Chief Constable Cheney attacks Home Office'. Cheney is reported to have said:

> I have been so proud of commanding the Buckinghamshire constabulary. It is second to none in England. It is up-to-date and efficient … Surely to command, one must try to know every individual and their wives and children. Then we can sort out worries and welfare problems. In this new amalgamation this cannot be done … I suppose it is unusual for an officer to attack policy in this way but I feel pretty strongly about this. I can see no advantage at all.

On 14 October Michael Larcombe, happy to have a roof over his head, celebrated his twenty-seventh birthday in Oxford prison. A week later, on the 21 October, the Aberfan disaster in South Wales dominated the headlines in the national newspapers. One hundred and forty-four people died when heavy rain caused a coal tip above the village of Aberfan in Wales to slide down the mountain, engulfing a farm, a school and several houses. No one ever expected this type of thing to happen. The feeling of being numbed, that so many innocents had been drowned or suffocated in mud, was widespread. The public had become used to being fed high death tolls from war films, but Aberfan was different: it was a new generation, domestic and televised.

On 12 November, a dozen or so civil offenders in B Wing at Oxford prison, including Michael Larcombe, were sitting around enjoying mugs of tea and reading the newspapers. The news that dominated the front page of the *Oxford Mail* that weekend was the motiveless murder of Dr Helen Davidson, in Hodgemoor Wood near Amersham. 'I had been transferred to B Wing in Oxford prison when the hospital cell on the top floor had become vacant,' Michael said:

It was lovely and warm. In the next cell was an Indian prisoner who was nearing the end of his sentence. He had sex with me. He had been serving a seven-year sentence for raping a girl at knifepoint. I was a criminal offender and was about to be transferred to an open prison but it was decided that as it was so close to my release date they scrapped it. So I came out about the end of November 1966. I'd served about four months of a six-month sentence for stealing a van, petrol and money from a garage in Amersham. I got out early on good behaviour. I stood outside, the prison door slamming shut behind me, with a couple of pounds in my pocket, a meal voucher, nowhere really to go and the weather deteriorating. A woman welfare worker in charge of a hostel in Oxford behind the prison was supposed to have collected me and taken me there but her husband had died the day before so I had to make my own way. I wasn't happy, it was very cold in the hostel bedroom, and was only there about a fortnight. I decided to pack my few belongings and left. I was out on the streets again. I thought I'd thumb down to the West Country, try and get some washing up in a hotel, somewhere to hide for the winter. I did get to Penzance in an articulated lorry delivering magazines and periodicals around the Cornish coast. The driver was ever so friendly. I remember staying in Newquay a few nights; I had a little money and did bed and breakfast.

It was the winter and I was on the road again thumbing. People were good to me – I got on well hitching lifts. When I had my Ford 500cwt Thames van that I'd bought with the compensation money from the accident I used to

give people lifts. In June 1961 I suffered head injuries in a
road crash in Amersham, which had left me facially mutilated and permanently brain damaged. Basically, I'd begun
an unstoppable sex change, swinging from being a man to
a woman. All this nine months after my 21st birthday. I've
lived with a hidden compulsion to dress up as a woman
for over fifty years now. My family must have felt bereavement – the loss of a son, the young man they had brought
into the world. The medical profession didn't understand.
After Newquay I found my way to mum and dad's home
in Somerset. They had moved from their council house in
Milton Road in Chesham before I was put in prison and
settled in a village on the outskirts of Chard in their own
semi. It was about 6 in the evening and dark when I reached
Chard. I went round to Woolworth's and could see father's
beige Ford Anglia. I walked towards them, the car shot
forward, they were going home. I knocked on the door. We
didn't say a lot. Mother said father wanted to talk to me.
He was listening to classical music. He was quite blunt and
said 'I don't care if you spend the rest of your life in prison.
I never want to see you again. Get out of my house', and
shut the door on me.

I tramped over Dartmoor with no food, no money,
nothing. I ended up in a church near a roundabout in the
centre of Weston Super Mare, worn out. I had holes in my
shoes and was wet through. The vicar found me. He was
ever so good and put me up in his flat for a couple of days,
then found me a place in a church army hostel in Bristol
that had individual bedrooms. I remember while I was there
seeing *Dr Zhivago*. I signed on at the labour exchange but
wasn't well enough for work, was acutely feminine and
couldn't settle. I went back to Weston Super Mare to the

church and told the vicar I was changing into a girl. He said,
'I'm referring you to the Mendip psychiatric hospital.' He
took me in his car past the Cheddar Gorge to the hospital
that was outside Wells on the Bath road for people suffering
from mental illness. I was classified as a voluntary patient.
I spent the Christmas of 1966 there and was there for the
next seventeen years. Throughout my whole time there
I was so ill because of everything, and they were putting
drugs into my food, androgens and male hormones. My
body was smashed apart. The accident changed everything.
I always had responsible jobs in the Mendip though, cutting
up grapefruit and sugaring them, making beds, changing
sheets once a week and serving meals on the trolley. Then
I started in the industrial therapy department packing Max
Factor gift sets. I earned £1.50 a week and was there about
two years and packed 30,000 gift sets. I used to put letters in
them saying I'd packed it and 'This gift set is finest quality.
I know – I packed it. I'd love to hear from you.' I had some
lovely replies. Then I started working as a ward orderly until
I got gallstones.

Dr Branson, at the Mendip, made an appointment for me
at the Bristol Royal Infirmary. At that time what I had was
swept under the carpet. I saw the specialist. If he'd offered
me a sex change I would have accepted. I was 27.

During our first telephone conversation in the spring of 2010,
Michael Larcombe told me of the joy he felt for the lifeline
he'd been given to tell his story. He was 71 and had dreamt for
fifty years of this day. Gradually over a period of three years he
told me the story of his life.

12

Treated as Suspects

'Despite the murder being on our doorstep, I wasn't aware of where exactly it had taken place. I never went into the woods to see where it happened. I couldn't even tell you which side of Bottrells Lane Dr Davidson's body was found', said Barbara Cox. Since 1950 Barbara and her husband had farmed 200 acres at Lower Bottom Farm, in Lower Bottom Lane. The lane was a long, narrow and just about passable track off the northern side of Bottrells Lane, leading to the junction with the A413 London Road – Amersham to the left and Chalfont St Giles to the right. The Cox's farm was barely two miles from the crime scene in Hodgemoor Wood but Barbara considered that outside her territory. 'I don't think I've ever walked in Hodgemoor Wood because we had our own woodland to walk in on our farm,' she said:

It had been a very different experience to have a quiet, gentle lady doctor. I was a mum with three small children and saw Dr Davidson over the years mainly for the children's immunisations. After she was murdered it's almost as if my own consciousness didn't want to know. Although I should have cared, it was nothing to do with me. We had to get on with our lives. The whole feeling then was, it's happened, it's all very sad, and there must have been a reason for it. My husband was interviewed at some stage by the police, along with other farmers, who all used to do their silage together and share the big farming equipment around here. He wasn't the sort of person to get involved and would only answer questions where necessary. Funnily enough I don't remember any conversations at home about the murder. Perhaps it was a bit close for comfort and the men didn't want us scared stiff. Local people wanted to be left alone. We didn't want all these intrusions from the police. I know the day the doctor was murdered she somehow reached a point near to the charcoal burner's site. Hazel Pearce from Stockings Farm used to say the police, early on, tried to pin it on the charcoal burner. Well they would if they could have done. It was really unfair on the poor chap.

The chief investigating officer, Det Ch Supt Jack Williams of Scotland Yard, told the press two weeks after the murder that the police were making progress and were close to making an arrest. It was a public relations exercise. The truth was that no new information had emerged. The police had run out of leads. It was obvious by its absence in the newspapers that neither police nor journalists were digging into a possible background story. Unsurprisingly, the police did not find the killer. They'd done their job, pulled in men, making many feel scared and guilty. Even the highly respected local GP, Dr John Rolt, Dr Davidson's partner at the Gore Hill medical practice, felt uncomfortable. According to Mrs Pauline Willes of the Old

Rectory in Chalfont St Giles, Dr Rolt, whom she consulted privately, thought he was a suspect for a while. She said, 'My husband and I socialised with Dr Rolt at various functions like the odd cocktail party or Christmas party. He thought he was a suspect for some while. He told me he felt like an accused man.' Mrs Willes couldn't explain the reason he felt he was a suspect other than he was a member of the same GP practice as Dr Davidson.

Dr John Baynton Rolt was 64. He was tall, distinguished looking, well spoken, regarded as a gentleman and was a long-standing member of the Chiltern Medical Society. As well as driving a Rolls-Royce, he was a sportsman, enjoyed shooting and when it was the shooting season he would take days off work. People thought highly of him. He was the senior partner at the Gore Hill medical practice with just a handful of NHS patients there, but with a long list of influential private patients who consulted him at Nightingales, his home in Cokes Lane, Chalfont St Giles where he lived with his wife Willa Mae, whom he married in 1937. He had a professional and friendly relationship with Dr Helen Davidson. Together they financed the building of the new medical practice in Gore Hill, in 1956, and he kept a framed, portrait photograph of her on the wall of his consulting room there.

Dr Rolt may have felt like a suspect but the police allowed him free access to Bottrells Lane. He was not stopped once as he drove his black Rolls-Royce along the lane when others were being questioned on every trip. Without the help of police records, I traced some of the innocent suspects the police interviewed, who felt they had been harassed by the investigation team.

The Estate Ranger's Story

On 14 November, five days after the murder and three days after the first reports about the murder began appearing in the press, the police left two notes under a dustbin lid outside the back door at Meadow Cottage, the home of Lloyd and Joyce King and their daughter Hilary. Lloyd was an estate ranger at Buckinghamshire County Council. Written on scraps torn from a lined notepad, and with illegible signatures, the notes were waiting for Lloyd when he returned home from work. One read: 'Mr Lloyd King, Please be at Amersham Police Station at 7.00 p.m. this evening (Monday).' The other note said: 'Mr Lloyd King, Please call at Stockings Farm, As soon as possible.'

Mrs Joyce King spent the afternoon of Wednesday 9 November in the kitchen at Meadow Cottage making a Christmas cake. She remembered:

> It was a horrible dismal day. I had been to work in the morning at Chesham Cottage Hospital where I was a nursing auxiliary. Lloyd usually finished work at five but came home early, about half past three, and offered to fetch our daughter Hilary in the car from school. She went to Challoner's Grammar school in Amersham. The next day … I always had Thursday off and Lloyd wasn't working that day. We looked out of the kitchen window and saw people walking in a row like on a TV police search. Lloyd decided to go across to Stockings Farm, the neighbouring farm, to ask our friend Phil Pearce if he knew what was happening. On his way one of the cadet soldiers carrying out the search spoke to Lloyd. They were looking for a lady who'd been birdwatching and was missing. My husband told him

exactly where birdwatchers went and that they needed to look on the other side of the road in Hodgemoor Wood because that's where they went. It was his undoing.

Lloyd's helpful remark to the cadet was misconstrued as guilt and taken as an indication he knew about the murder. He was treated as a suspect:

The police officer said Lloyd had told the soldier 'they should look over there and that they'd find her over there'. Lloyd had said something in good faith which when repeated to the police sounded suspicious. He wasn't clever enough with words to fight back at the police. He was honest.

The police called him first over to Stockings Farm. They used one of the rooms and questioned him there, then at Amersham police station more than once. Williams of Scotland Yard questioned him. He said something like 'Come on laddie. Tell us where you did it. Tell us why you did it. It will be a lot easier for you if you tell us. Just admit it.' They gave him a rough time. I can remember Lloyd coming in the back door. He was bright red. He rarely saw bad in anyone but said: 'If they make you feel like this when you're innocent, whatever must it feel like if you're guilty.' My husband couldn't kill a mouse. He didn't know how to lie. They scared him. He was a gentle quiet man who kept his emotions to himself. The fact he had been interviewed by the police was enough to make him feel guilty.

He found the police very rude but after the last interview at Amersham police station that was it. They didn't hound him any more. They knew it couldn't have been Lloyd because he had an alibi with Hilary being collected from school. But for several days police were at the entrance of our drive and questioned us each time we came home. Although they knew us they never once let us go without the same questions. They were just playing at it because they knew who we were. We used to come down the drive to go to Amersham to take Hilary to school, and when I went to work, and the police were there. Each time they stopped us they wanted identification. It seemed to go on for ages. We watched over our daughter Hilary but because we were so far off the beaten track she could not come and go without us driving her. We were naturally curious to know who did it and why, and that he or she should not go unpunished. It was a big event. But we were both too busy earning our living to really let it affect our lives. After all this time I only remember the facts. I imagine they cornered everyone that lived locally. The charcoal burners were the ones who were highlighted at the time.

Phil Pearce's daughter, Rosalind, at Stockings Farm said, 'The laughable thing is that the police didn't pick up Lloyd and question him until November 14, by which time we [Lloyd King and his daughter Hilary and Rosalind and her father] had already visited the murder site.'

The Charcoal Burner's Story

The police pointed accusing fingers at David Mulkern, the charcoal burner. He was a suspect because of his workplace's proximity to the scene of the crime in Hodgemoor Wood and because of the burnt and bloody appearance of a length of

wood found fairly close to Dr Davidson's body and presumed
to be the murder weapon. In the secret post-mortem report,
forensic pathologist Dr David Bowen described it as wood
from a bonfire which was not the same as 'black wood', a by-
product of charcoal burning in a cauldron.

'The police were an absolute pain in the arse,' said Mulkern.
'We had policemen every day in Bottrells Lane, stopping
every vehicle, except for the man with the Rolls-Royce who
came in the Magpie pub on the Beaconsfield road near the
western end of Bottrells Lane. He told us they didn't stop him.'
Mulkern was referring to Dr John Rolt, one of Dr Davidson's
practice partners, who regularly drove along Bottrells Lane to
his home in Chalfont St Giles:

> They stopped me every day as if I was someone new. Each
> time they asked me where I was going. The day the murder
> happened I was delivering charcoal to Bow in London.
> My wife came with me. In the '60s I spent a lot of hours
> going to restaurants. The Angus Steak Houses used charcoal
> for barbecuing meat. Police, plain clothes detectives, high-
> ranking, they all came to the house and insisted I go to
> the police station. I went to the new police station in top
> Amersham and was put in an office with five detectives
> that sat round me, throwing questions right, left and centre.
> No stone was left unturned, they gave me a good grilling.
> 'Why did you do it?' they kept asking me. I was extremely
> annoyed. We had delivered to the Angus Steak House in
> Bow on the day of the murder. It had taken all day. He, the
> managing director of the steak house, was a magistrate. The
> police could have saved themselves their effort, and me the
> aggravation, if they'd checked. I read them the riot act, told
> them their fortune, and that if they couldn't be bothered to

check my alibi they were wasting their time. They upset my mother. A young chap called Lloyd King got quite a grilling. They threw a lot of resources at it. The police had done their job and made me feel guilty. They did pester quite a few people, local workers. They searched my brother-in-law's flat and took his clothes and tools away.

The Cesspit Cleaner's Story

Pat Drew lived in Piggot's Orchard, the council estate on Gore Hill next to Dr Davidson's medical practice. From the front door she could look straight down to the bus garage to their canteen and the office where passengers went for timetable information. Pat's father, Norman Collins, worked for Amersham District Council as a full-time cesspool lorry driver, driving from the council depot in Old Amersham to the outlying villages of Coleshill and Winchmore Hill. Norman Collins was helped by his mate, Mr Neilson. Before mains drainage and inside lavatories came to villages, properties had cesspits or septic tanks. Their sewerage was cleaned then disgorged by big, green 'stink lorries' as they were known locally, into underground pits in Pipers Wood. It was the foulest of jobs.

On 9 November, Collins and Neilson had their sandwich lunch as usual in the lay-by where Dr Davidson would later leave her car. Mrs Drew said:

> The police questioned both of them. The only thing that comes to mind, they cross-questioned my father's mate longer than my father. He was younger and came from up

North and worked with father for several years. The police
came to the house and father had to go to the police station
with them. Mother was very worried and got flustered.
Everybody was pointing fingers at everybody, suspecting
everyone else of the murder. There was a dread of what
people on the estate would think if they knew the family
had been questioned by the police. They were questioning
men in general.

The Motorcyclist's Story

Det Sgt Tony Dale said the unnamed motorcyclist was a
suspect, but not for long. Michael Larcombe's name was added
to the list of men to be questioned by the police. It would
probably have been at the top of the list of suspects as he had a
grievance against the doctor. Five years earlier, Dr Davidson's
skilful defence team had quashed the careless driving charge
against her. Larcombe had an axe to grind. He had wanted
Dr Davidson to behave honourably and admit the car crash in
1961 was her fault. He told me himself he would have killed
her on her doorstep if the opportunity had arisen. Did he have
the opportunity to commit murder? There was an importance
in the timing of the murder. Larcombe had a cast-iron alibi for
9 November 1966. He was safely locked up in Oxford prison,
serving the last part of a six-month sentence:

> I can remember sitting on a bunk bed and saw one of the
> others had the *Oxford Mail* that weekend. The headlines
> about Dr Davidson's murder didn't register to begin with.
> I couldn't believe it. Only her violent death gave me the

courage to go on living. Later in the cold light of day I was ever so upset. No police officers came to question me.

On checking the motorcyclist's whereabouts, Tony Dale said the police had learned the young man was 'on remand'. He said, 'The motorcyclist's social worker worked in an office two doors along from Chesham nick. His name was Smith. A nice man and the best probation officer I've ever come across.' We now know Larcombe was actually locked up in Oxford prison serving a six-month sentence for stealing a van and money from B&M Motors in Amersham. Larcombe told me he could not remember a social worker called Smith. His alibi must have come as a blow to the murder investigation team.

Herbert Baker

Helen Davidson's husband, Herbert Baker, would be the obvious first suspect. On the morning of Friday 18 November 1966, Mrs Herriot, a patient of Dr Davidson and whose husband was an engineer at Amersham Hospital, was travelling on a single-decker bus from Chesham to Winchmore Hill, three and a half miles south-west of Amersham. She picked up a folded copy of that day's *Bucks Examiner* that had been left on the seat. The front page was devoted to the Dr Davidson story. There were photographs of Helen Davidson, Ch Con Brig John Cheney and Det Ch Supt Jack Williams of Scotland Yard. At the top right-hand corner, above the headline 'BRUTAL MURDER IN HODGEMOOR WOOD', a message had been written in biro. It read, 'Why don't you question the husband more?' Mrs Herriot recalled:

It gave me the shivers. I don't know where I'd been but I got off the bus and took it to the police station straight away. I thought it strange. Why should somebody write that? Somebody must have known something. The police told me they had questioned the husband a lot and that he had reported her missing some hours after she hadn't arrived home. The policeman said the husband did seem to have left it a long time, but he was not involved in the murder. I couldn't believe she'd been murdered. I'd seen her about a week before she died. She seemed just the same, a bit abrupt, but very nice.

The police had been quick to dismiss Mrs Herriot's information. Had the *Bucks Examiner* been left intentionally on the seat or by accident? A wife or husband is always the obvious suspect. Was it a ploy to cast suspicion on someone else diverting attention from the real killer? Was it someone who wanted to discredit a decent man, make trouble for Herbert Baker and deliberately left on the seat for that purpose? Was it the work of a prankster?

Tony Dale had said: 'You always start with the closest to the victim. He was grilled inside and out … and totally ruled out. He would have provided a satisfactory explanation as to where he was that afternoon and was not involved in the murder.' Something, however, was wrong with Baker's delay in reporting his wife's disappearance to the police on the evening of 9 November. It was only with reluctance he called them late that night. Why? There could be an innocent explanation but it looked suspicious. Was Baker used to his wife's late returns from her Wednesday walks? Did he confide in the police about Helen's fugues, from which she had occasionally suffered since the car crash in 1961 and resulted in her losing track of time?

Did he deliberately withhold this background information? Either way, the longer he waited to call the police that night, the more confusion would be created over the time of the doctor's death. Baker was quick to forgive the killer. I thought it strange that he could preach forgiveness on Remembrance Sunday, four days after his wife's murder. It was almost as if he knew something.

What proof did the police have that Baker's testimony about the last morning he and his wife spent together was true? His words were taken at face value. How reliable were the recollections of this 80-year-old gentleman? He had told the police he and Helen had done gardening together that morning but did not mention the home visit she made to a patient in Hyde Heath. It may have been an oversight on his part but what else did he leave out? And how did trained police officers miss this crucial detail? Did he actually arrive home from his part-time job at 5.30 p.m.? He may have had an alibi at work, but no apparent witness to his return home. The police only had his word.

Mrs Herriot, in whom Dr Davidson confided about her sudden and forthcoming marriage to Herbert Baker, said he had pushed the doctor into marriage. Had he intentionally set out to marry this not-for-marrying lady and move into Ashlyn, her beautiful home in Chesham Bois, in order to provide accommodation for his former housekeeper Kathleen Cook? Following the death of Kathleen's foster mother, Annie Eldridge in January 1961, and the subsequent sale of Fairview, her house in Hyde Heath, Kathleen became homeless. On Baker's marriage to Dr Davidson, Rosemead conveniently passed into the hands of Kathleen Cook.

There is evidence to show police swiftly dismissed any involvement Herbert Baker may have had with the crime. But did they ask him 'Who will benefit from your wife's death?'

Baker would definitely have benefitted. So too, eventually, would her adversary Kathleen Cook.

The Housekeeper

The animosity between Kathleen Cook and Helen Davidson was obvious. Kathleen was described by a Hyde Heath resident as 'the murderess', but few in the village would speak openly to me about rumours in 1966 concerning her involvement in the doctor's murder. The police though had made the connection. The local press reported the official line that Helen Davidson had been struck over the head by a length of burnt timber found not far from the body. But behind the scenes the police suspected Kathleen's involvement and dug up her garden at Rosemead in search of a murder weapon. Was their search thorough? They did not check inside the septic tank in the garden. Was she adequately questioned? Kathleen had a motive for killing the doctor: jealousy. She had been loyal to Herbert Baker, like a wife, for more than twenty years, while his first wife's health deteriorated. She couldn't imagine a life without Herbert Baker, had not welcomed his second marriage and resented Dr Davidson. She had set her sights on Herbert and saw her home and future inheritance from him being handed over to his new wife. With the doctor dead, Rosemead would definitely be hers. After Herbert Baker's death in January 1975, didn't the police realise that beneficiaries from this elderly gentleman's will written in 1971 may have had some bearing on a possible motive for his wife's murder? Kathleen Cook stood to benefit from half of Baker's estate that he had inherited from Kathleen's rival, Helen Davidson. It was suspicious.

The Amersham Garage Bus Driver

Bus driver George Garbett was a person of habit. After finishing his shift on the Green Line coach out of Amersham bus garage he would always drive home to Chalfont St Giles via the scenic route, heading south on the A355 via the narrow, winding and steep Gore Hill, turning left into Bottrells Lane and past the lovers' car parks either side of the lane close to Stockings Farm. At the end of the lane, after a further three quarters of a mile, he took a right turn into Silver Hill and right again into School Lane down to Well Cottage on the left, opposite the village school. It was almost a mile further than the direct route to Chalfont St Giles, south east along the A413 London Road from Amersham. On Wednesday 9 November 1966, Garbett was working on the early shift, 7 a.m. to 3 p.m., out of the bus garage.

13

In the Frame

Dr Helen Davidson was familiar to nearly everyone in Amersham. She was also a lady of habit. For the ten years that her medical practice had been located at the bottom of Gore Hill it was generally known to workers at the bus garage opposite that Wednesdays were Dr Davidson's day off – they would have noticed that her car, originally a Morris 1000 Traveller, then a Hillman Minx, was not parked in the surgery car park, a distance of about twenty-five yards away.

George Garbett, London Transport bus driver number N1167, drove a Green Line coach out of Amersham bus garage. Green Line Coaches were part of the London Transport Executive, a large, powerful and respected bus company, which dominated the scene at the Broadway end of Old Amersham. The bus garage was one of the town's biggest employers and the hub of the town. Buses were the town's lifeblood, ferrying passengers to schools, work, cinemas and dances at weekends. They arrived and departed to strict timetables, known off by heart by passengers and overseen by the acting chief inspector of the garage, William Evans.

Garbett was the same age as Helen Davidson, but that's where the similarity ended. Whereas she was loved by nearly everyone, had influence and confidence, he was a man of humble means with no friends: a loner. He had never been part of the garage community that treated bus driving as less of a job and more like a family concern, where there was a real feeling of belonging. While most Amersham bus crews enjoyed dances and buses down to the coast, cricket matches, darts, all manner of social things, some found it difficult to socialise, George Garbett being one of them. To look at him you would never know he had a problem, but he had actually been damaged during the Second World War. He had sustained serious head injuries following a road traffic accident whilst serving in the army as a motorbike despatch rider. It resulted in him needing a metal plate inserted into his skull to protect his brain.

He had come to Amersham after the war, where he could earn slightly more money driving what were considered to be the more classy Green Line coaches than the buses in his hometown of Tonbridge in Kent. It was about the same time as Helen Davidson began her career as a GP in the town. Garbett lodged then with a man called Harry Sharp, in a small terraced property called Homeleigh in Station Road, two doors away from the famous Rep. Theatre. The White House, a fine period house which was Helen Davidson's first home in parallel Church Street in Old Amersham, was a distance of just under a mile from Homeleigh, separated only by Rectory Wood. In the late 1940s, Dr Davidson shared the house with Miss Eve White and the recently qualified GP Dr David Howell and his wife Rosemary.

From 1953 until his marriage in September 1956 at Tonbridge Register Office in Kent to divorcee Edna Williams, Garbett, a bachelor until the age of 39, rented a three-bedroomed house in the Weller Road council estate in Amersham on the hill where he had lived alone, keeping himself to himself. It was due to be repossessed for a family's occupation. George Garbett and Edna Williams were both 39, considered middle-aged then. Edna previously worked in an exclusive draper's shop in Tunbridge Wells but after her marriage to George became a bus conductress at Amersham bus garage. Two years later, the six-week-long London Transport bus strike was crippling the capital. In the middle of June 1958, not one bus left any London Transport Executive garage, the unions claim for 25*s* more on their £10-a-week salaries had been rejected and there was job insecurity. George Garbett was one driver who was badly affected. In 1959, however, despite London Transport's ruling that bus drivers were not supposed to be employed in other capacities, he was grateful to be engaged as a live-in gardener-cum-chauffeur with an extra £3 a week cash in hand, by Douglas and Pauline Willes. They were a well-to-do couple who had recently moved from Cokes Lane in Amersham to the Old Rectory in Dean Way in the picturesque, ancient village of Chalfont St Giles. On the corner of Dean Way and School Lane, the late seventeenth-century two-storey detached house of elegant proportions was set in a large garden and protected from the main road by the long brick wall of their barn which had been converted into garaging for three cars. A gravel drive separated the two buildings. Pauline Willes told me they had only heard the Old Rectory was for sale because she and her husband were friends with the Rector of Amersham and 'the Rector told me it was coming on the market. But it didn't. We bought it direct from the Church Commissioners.'

In the 1950s, Chalfont St Giles, on the edge of the Chiltern Hills, was a long, narrow, not over-friendly village from where

City workers commuted to London. Its centre was a high street lined with timber-framed cottages that widened to a small village green with a duck pond and the twelfth-century Chalfont St Giles parish church. There was an acute national housing shortage after the Second World War, so Garbett was fortunate to have the security of a cottage that came with the job. In return for the gardening work at the Old Rectory, he and Edna were given Well Cottage, a tied gardener's cottage, rent-free. It had previously been a run-down dwelling that had been cleaned and whitewashed inside and stood hidden behind the high red-brick garden wall of the Old Rectory at the bottom of School Lane. A solid wooden door in the wall of the lane opened directly into the garden making it easy for George to come and go without being seen by anyone in the big house.

Douglas Willes was a high-ranking member of the establishment and belonged to Prince Philip's Royal Yacht Squadron on the Isle of Wight, the most exclusive yacht club in the UK and which was joined by invitation only. That meant you needed to have been around the sailing fraternity a while and become known to existing members. Membership of the club was regarded as something of a privilege for the 'right sort' of person, upper-middle class at least, and often retired senior officers in the armed forces. Mr Willes's sister, Rosemary, was married to Dr David Howell, Dr Davidson's practice partner: 'If I wished to consult a lady doctor privately I would ask Dr Davidson to call at the house,' said Mrs Willes. 'I obviously wouldn't want to see my brother-in-law Dr Howell about anything personal.'

The new position with the Willes family suited George Garbett. He often worked split shifts at the bus garage, during the early morning and evening peaks. During the long break in the middle of the day he could now undertake more gardening work. During one telephone conversation, Mrs Willes told me, 'When George came to us he wasn't a trained gardener but he was good at his job. He only did so many hours gardening.' What Mrs Willes didn't know was that George had learnt his gardening skills as a child in the 1920s. He had attended school in East Peckham, a remote country village on the edge of the Weald of Kent, where the head-master, Mr Pope, had placed great emphasis on gardening. Because of the food crisis following the First World War, the teaching of gardening received an enormous stimulus owing to the necessity for producing food from all available land. The keeping of a well-cropped, well-planned and clean garden was judged to be of considerable educational value. A county gardening inspector called frequently for discussions with the headmaster and made long reports in the school logbook.

On Wednesday 9 November 1966 Garbett was working on the early shift out of Amersham bus garage. Each bus driver knew the structure of their rotas at least thirty-nine days in advance. Their lives on the buses, whether one-man operated, crew operated or Green Line drivers, were governed by time-tables. Garbett knew therefore that he was on the rota to drive his coach route number 710, the only Green Line coach running out of Amersham then, between 7 a.m. and 3 p.m. on 9 November. Despite the usual traffic jams in and out of London on the sixty-mile round trip, he arrived back in Amersham not long after 3 p.m. After completing his shift he signed off and his conductor paid in their takings. The records of his shift that day, by some twist of fate, are now missing from London Transport archives. Garbett then left the garage in his old Hillman Minx car and took his usual route home to Chalfont St Giles.

It seems unusual that Garbett, who had lived in Amersham since the end of the Second World War, and who regularly

drove home along Bottrells Lane, worked directly opposite
Dr Davidson's surgery at Amersham bus garage and lived
approximately one mile from the murder site in Chalfont
St Giles in a property owned by Mr and Mrs Willes, was
not questioned by the police. There, in the background, and
known to Dr David Howell (the Willes's brother-in-law) and
his general practice partner Dr Helen Davidson, who regularly
visited the Old Rectory for medical, social or family reasons,
was Geoge Garbett the resident gardener. All these facts should
have put him in the frame. He was an obvious suspect.

According to published reports, 2,000 men were questioned, and statements taken. The police stopped nearly
everyone driving along Bottrells Lane. I assume they stopped
Garbett. He had driven along the lane in the middle of the
afternoon on 9 November. Did he not raise any suspicions?
Surely he was flagged up as at least being close to the murder
scene at the time of the doctor's death. He was also someone
who may have known that Wednesday was her day off. But
then the police were not looking for anyone who may have
had the opportunity to commit murder, only at the lack of
motive. They were convinced it was a random killing to the
exclusion of everything else. All avenues of investigation were
not explored.

I asked Det Sgt Tony Dale to clarify why the bus driver had
not even been questioned. He repeated that the man whose
name he didn't remember who lived in a cottage in Chalfont
St Giles, the address of which he didn't remember 'didn't
figure in the murder … the police had no cause to suspect
him … nothing to indicate he was of interest'. The police, it
would seem, made no effort to investigate the movements of
George Garbett or his background. He slipped through the
net. I wondered what sort of family he came from.

Garbett's parents were similar to many other working-class families. At the turn of the twentieth century, George's father Hubert, aged 15, travelled south from Shropshire where he had been a farm labourer, to London in search of a better life. He did well for himself. He was employed firstly as a footman then promoted to butler to John Henry Nelson, a gentleman of independent means. In 1911 he left the Nelson household to open a grocer's shop in the downstairs of a Victorian terraced house in Wandle Road, the lower-class end of Wimbledon in south-west London. In 1914 he married Jane Beatrice Ironside, a lady's maid. Their son, George, was born in 1917. The First World War prematurely ended Hubert's life as a master grocer. In 1917, aged 30, he enlisted as a private in the 1st Battalion 5th Division East Surrey Regiment. He went with his battalion to Bombay, then to operations north of Baghdad, his regiment later being retained as a unit of the Army of Occupation in Mesopotamia, the ancient name for Iraq. Nothing prepared him for the conditions there, which defied description. Operations were carried out in intense heat, often in mountainous regions by men who had done little training. There were high casualty rates amongst British troops, particularly from faulty ammunition, some of which was supplied by Eley Brothers. The arid desert, flooding, flies and vermin led to appalling levels of sickness and death. Medical arrangements were shocking. He saw frightened faces, suffering not only of the body but of the mind, and death.

By August 1919, the unrest in Hubert's battalion was disturbing the men's minds. He was discharged in March 1920. Like millions he was a changed man. He had lived through the nightmare of the most devastating war in history, the England he fought for no longer existed and he was a stranger in his own home. A million men died, 2 million were wounded and the crippled and maimed 'heroes' begged on street corners. Despite shortages of just about everything – food, coal, petrol, paper – Hubert luckily secured a position as butler to Col Sir Henry Streatfeild at Chiddingstone House in Kent. Sir Henry, a regimental commander of the Grenadier Guards during the First World War, was private secretary to Queen Alexandra. The queen, by coincidence, was a member of the elite Royal Skating Club of which Alan Davidson, Helen Davidson's father, was a member. Hubert's world now concentrated in serving gentry, royalty and politicians. George's older sister, Elsie, aged 5, died six months after Hubert's discharge from the army. His brother Frank was born in 1921. By 1925, aged 40 and still suffering the ravages of wartime, Hubert left service. With no apparent source of income the Garbetts turned to taking in lodgers, mainly police officers from the local police station, at a house they rented in Tonbridge in Kent. In 1955, Jane Garbett moved into a council house in Tonbridge but Hubert, who had acute depression, was admitted to a mental asylum where he remained until his death in 1964.

On the morning of 10 November 1966, while the police searched for Helen Davidson, Mrs Pauline Willes of the Old Rectory had driven west from Chalfont St Giles along Bottrells Lane in the direction of the main Amersham to Beaconsfield road. She said:

> I was driving through the cut [Bottrells Lane] and the police stopped me and asked if I'd seen the doctor's car or anybody. They hadn't found her body. It was Dr Rolt that later told me Dr Davidson had been murdered. I don't think the murder impinged on our lives much. It was a bit of a storm in a teacup.

Chalfont St Giles had its own local police officer, who lived in
a police house in the village and was involved in local doorstep
enquiries. Mrs Willes said 'I didn't hear anything of a door-to-
door search in the village. The police certainly didn't come to
our door.'

On 1 January 1970, London Transport's Green Line Coaches
were hived off to form London Country Bus Services. George
Garbett was one of the long-serving drivers at Amersham
bus garage who was at an age when it was difficult to change
habits of a lifetime. He couldn't face working for a brand-new
company and chose to be transferred to Uxbridge garage,
about six miles away, to stay with London Transport for a
higher salary, taking with him his seniority and also his loyalty
to the company.

At our meeting in 2009, Det Sgt Tony Dale had told me of
the unnamed bus driver who killed himself some years after
the murder of Dr Davidson. He'd said to me that it wasn't
until the bus driver's suicide that the facts of how he began
unburdening his guilt to his GP came to light. Dale said:

> I can remember sitting in that doctor's surgery with another
> police officer and can still see the doctor disclosing all those
> details about his patient, the bus driver, about a week after
> he committed suicide. He told us that in his opinion this
> could well be the man who murdered Helen Davidson. He
> gave us intimate details he had discussed with the bus driver
> about being bisexual, impotent and with a strong sexual
> urge. He said the bus driver was schizophrenic and it was a
> very dangerous combination. For the bus driver talking to
> the doctor it was like lifting the lid off his conscience. The
> doctor said these people guide you towards something then
> retract. He [the bus driver] was trying to tell the doctor

something but couldn't. He didn't want to admit it but would deny murdering the woman when nobody was suggesting it. In other words the bus driver wanted to be asked more about the murder. He was trying to nudge the doctor in the right direction and get him to drag something out of him. He was getting nearer and nearer. He had something on his conscience about a woman. The doctor was in no doubt that the bus driver could well be the killer. He was a shrewd bloke. He knew the man was going to confess and was getting close to it.

Garbett's sister-in-law knew very little about her husband Frank's older brother. She rarely saw him. 'We weren't close. Sometimes we met at Christmas or in the summer. George didn't get on with Frank.' She recalled that George took pride in his appearance and showed no signs of his wartime brain injury. Then out of the blue she mentioned that 'George was not a mummy's boy'. This was an old-fashioned phrase used to describe someone who was a homosexual, which in those days would have been shameful. Was George's sister-in-law subconsciously unburdening the Garbett secret? George's well-groomed façade concealed a complex, less accommodating personality that he had been privately living with for over twenty years in the form of mental illness.

Presumably the GP, in whom George confided in the early 1970s, knew of his wartime brain injury. However, as the curator of the Army Medical Museum told me, the National Health Service did not come into existence until 1948, so it is probable that details of Garbett's brain injury may not have been included on his medical record. Many wartime records were destroyed and those that did survive did so by chance. George Garbett was a loner. He had a history of sexual failure. He was distressed by his inability to sustain a satisfactory relationship with a woman. His homosexuality could explain his marriage at the age of 39 that never was: he needed respectability.

By the early 1970s, five years after the murder of Dr Davidson, the troubled and guilt-ridden George Garbett had sought medical help. He was suffering emotional and sexual problems. He confided in his doctor who listened to his outpourings. Garbett had kept his cool for five years but wanted to be free of a terrible guilt, and unburden his conscience. He did not like the man he was seeing in the mirror. The millstone of his secret weighed heavily. Bit by bit, over a period of months, he told his confidant of his sexual failure, guilt, and how he had done something awful to a woman. The doctor said there were no voices in the man's head telling him he had done wrong, 'It was actual not imagined – he actually felt guilt.' He hadn't come to terms with the awful deed and was trying to escape from a situation that was intolerable. The doctor tried to break down the barrier to reveal his patient's problem.

George's doctor was faced with a dilemma. Should he report his patient to the police? But by so doing he would betray his doctor-patient confidentiality and, therefore, kept the matter secret.

Garbett's next appointment with his doctor was on Friday 23 July 1971. It was Garbett's day off. He had no intention of keeping the appointment. Instead he left his home, walked the few yards to the bottom of School Lane, turned left into Dean Way, left again into the gravel driveway of the Old Rectory, his employer's home, and took his 5-year-old Hillman Minx, similar to that owned by Dr Davidson, out of the first garage where he'd left it the night before. He parked it in front of the garage door and got out. Then in a dramatic suicide, having doused himself with petrol from a rusty can, he climbed into the front seat of the car and set fire to himself by lighting a match. Suicide by fire, known as self-immolation, is an uncommon and extreme way of committing suicide – rare in developed countries, more frequent in developing countries.

George Garbett saw in that moment all the dead and maimed whom he loved and missed: his sister who had died at the age of 4; he couldn't forget his mother Jane who had been a support to him, been his ally, kept his secret and who was an example to the Garbett family; his father Hubert who had served in the First World War and died two years previously in a mental hospital just six months after Jane's death. For George, mental illness was a family secret, a curse. There was an enormous stigma attached to having a relative in a mental hospital. It was anxiously concealed, out of sight out of mind. Garbett was 54, had felt the pain of guilt tearing him apart and died before anyone discovered his deadly secret, which he took to his grave.

Mrs Willes described how there was a loud explosion at about 10 a.m. that Friday. Reverend William Palmer's wife came rushing out from St Giles church, managing to stop Mrs Willes's daughter from seeing the horror of the scene: a charred body in a burning car. Mrs Willes said, 'George had hooked the exhaust into the inside of his old car, locked the door from the inside and had a knife with him as well which he didn't use, before setting fire to himself. He had tried once before to kill himself. He was obviously depressed.' The corpse was in a bad state. Garbett's body parts were so badly burnt in the fire that his widow Edna had to identify her husband by various articles of his clothing found in the car, that were shown to her by Con Michael Woolhouse. Con Woolhouse was the local intelligence officer with Amersham police responsible for collating information about local criminals, making sure police officers were up to date with their movements and anything else suspicious.

On George Garbett's death certificate an open verdict was given, ensuring that any life insurance policy George may have had, with the usual get-out clause for an act of suicide, would have been honoured. He died without leaving a will, had been sufficiently hard-up in his life to need two jobs and his salary as a bus driver by 1971 had only risen to £20 a week. Yet after probate he had over £2,400 in his bank account, which was a lot of money then – the equivalent of £25,000 in today's money. This was at a time when working-class people rarely left any money, and it was more than a bus driver would have been able to save in those days.

Only a few people attended the funeral service, officiated by Rev William Palmer at St Giles church in the village. Those that did attend included Mr and Mrs Willes, and Mary Grove who had been a bus conductress since the end of the Second World War and worked on the Green Line coach that George drove. He was cremated on 30 July 1971 at the Chiltern Crematorium, his ashes being dispersed in their Woodland Gardens of Remembrance. The death certificate stated his brain had coagulated. When Garbett intentionally burnt himself alive in his car he destroyed all evidence of himself, his personality disorder, and the wartime head injury described to me by his sister-in-law, which had required a steel plate inserted into his skull to protect his brain. This was an important fact unknown to the police.

George Garbett's doctor did not go to the police with his concerns and intimate details about his patient until after his suicide. It would have violated his oath of care and confidentiality. A week later he told Amersham police that in his opinion this was the man who may well have murdered Helen Davidson. The only real evidence of the conversations between Garbett and his GP is in medical files closed under the 100-year ruling. Other than his birth in Wimbledon in 1917, his marriage in Tonbridge in 1956 and his death in 1971 there was only a brief official glimpse of this Amersham bus driver's life in a five-line obituary in London Transport's staff magazine, and a write-up in the 29 July 1971 edition of *The Buckinghamshire Advertiser* about the sudden death of George Garbett the previous Friday morning, 23 July, and the 'accident' that killed him.

Was there any investigation to find possible connections between the arson attacks in Chesham in July 1966 in which 'HELP D.D.' had been intriguingly scrawled with a charred piece of wood on a wall of a property 100 yards from Chesham Cottage Hospital where Dr Davidson used to practise as an anaesthetist, the assumed burnt wood murder weapon, the illegal bonfires in Hodgemoor Wood, then George Garbett's suicide by self-immolation in Chalfont St Giles five years later? Did the murder investigation team not consider there may have been a connection? Despite the appearance of a thorough and ongoing investigation by the police they apparently had no reason to link this man with severe personality problems to the murder.

With criminal profiling now it would be easier to understand that a man with such symptoms, as described by the doctor whom Garbett consulted in 1971, could be capable of murder. He should have been a prime suspect. The pattern of his life was not dissimilar to that of his father, Hubert Garbett, who survived the horrors of the First World War, went back into service to serve the gentry and ended life in an asylum not to be seen again. George joined up, was injured during

the Second World War, went into service for Mr and Mrs
Willes and ended his life with mental health problems and
suicide. In 1966, the police immediately ruled out a sexual
motive in the murder of Dr Davidson as there had been no
sexual interference of the body. They were not sophisticated
in their enquiry methods then. Homosexuality, bisexuality,
impotency, schizophrenia and loner were merely words to
a police force that was not advanced in analysing criminal
behaviour. It may have been the Swinging Sixties for many,
but George Garbett was war damaged and this was not something the police force then would have understood. The war
had been over for twenty years but for some there were mis-
understood lasting effects.

One piece of information that had come to light in 1966
in *The Times* and London's *Evening Standard*, was that five
days after the murder, police photographers in a light aircraft
took aerial photographs of Hodgemoor Wood. Detectives had
asked for pictures showing little-used paths and glades to get
an idea of where the killer could walk and hide and see the
way he came and went. The area photographed included the
lay-by on the main road where Dr Davidson's car had been
found, the whole of the wood, and much of Bottrells Lane,
which leads to Chalfont St Giles. Although the woodland
didn't extend the entire length of the lane there were many
hidden footpaths and tracks that the attacker could have taken
without being seen. It would have been possible to approach
and escape from the murder scene through the woods parallel
to Bottrells Lane, then a short step across a field at the eastern
end of the lane to Chalfont St Giles.

On 9 November 1966, no one was seen parking near
the doctor's car in the lay-by on the B473 Amersham
to Beaconsfield road, and no one saw the doctor in

the woodland. If newspaper reports are to be believed – and the police for their own reasons weren't holding back any information – the only vehicles spotted in Bottrells Lane, and not accounted for at the alleged time the murder was committed, were a blue Ford Zephyr, a grey Vauxhall Viva and a green Austin truck. Which raises questions: did Garbett park his car in the lovers' car park in Bottrells Lane much later that afternoon *after* everyone had left Hodgemoor Wood? Any earlier and the car would probably have been noticed by walkers who had parked there and its presence reported to the police during the murder investigation. Or did Garbett drive straight home, park his car in his usual spot in his employer's garage at the Old Rectory in Chalfont St Giles, and make his way back into Hodgemoor Wood using the less public route, on foot? He knew his surroundings well. All he had to do afterwards was keep under cover most of the way home and nobody would have seen him. The answer will probably remain a mystery.

This question remains, however: why would Garbett kill Dr Davidson? The GP in whom Garbett confided could not of course give any detail as to how or why his patient was driven to kill. But with the profile described by the doctor, murder, it seems, given the right circumstances, was always a possibility. Was it a chance agonising confrontation on the afternoon of 9 November 1966? Did Helen Davidson find him in the darkness of the woods indulging in his murky world of unnatural acts and secret bonfires that gave him power? Garbett had been recognised by the doctor. For that, he hated her. In those awful moments he was filled with fear, lust and satisfaction. Fear that he would lose everything, his home, his job with the Willes family whom he respected and for whom he had worked for the last seven years, his job with London Transport. The fear that Helen Davidson, who had discovered the secret part of his life, would divulge it. Fear of his homosexuality, which was outside the law, being gossiped about at the bus garage – it would ruin him. He was a criminal in a vulnerable position. He had everything to lose. His life flashed before him. He snapped. Garbett knew he had to kill the doctor. He was a complex man. He didn't understand the confusion in his mind that had begun over twenty years earlier when the metal plate was inserted into his skull to protect his brain. He saw his own lust combined with impotence, then the satisfaction, enjoyment and the power he obtained from grinding the doctor's eyes into her skull. He had triumphed over a powerful woman. He saw his father before him, who had seen the horrors of the First World War, dying in a mental institution. Everything came together. War made George Garbett what he was.

Could the murder of Dr Davidson have been premeditated? Kathleen Cook had a motive for wanting the doctor dead. The police, by digging up her garden during the murder investigation, obviously suspected she had something to hide. Someone may have helped George Garbett with his blood-spattered clothes. Had she and Garbett somehow been thrown together during regular bus journeys that she took between Hyde Heath, Chesham Bois and Amersham? Garbett knew well in advance that he had a window of opportunity on 9 November. Kathleen was one of the only people capable of controlling Fancy, Dr Davidson's unpredictable and aggressive dog who would never allow anyone near his mistress. After the murder Kathleen looked after the dog at Rosemead in Hyde Heath until it died at an advanced age. Whether the murder of Dr Davidson was committed in a moment of madness or planned with precision, either way it seems no one in Chalfont St Giles made the connection between the murder in 1966 and George Garbett's suicide five years later. The opinion locally was that the suicide was hushed up.

Mrs Barbara Ogden, widow of Dr Bill Ogden who was a founder member and past president of the Chiltern Medical Society and in private practice with Dr Mike Webber in Chalfont St Peter, told me, 'One of the GPs in the society knew who murdered Dr Davidson.' Who else knew? Mrs Browne, widow of Ch Insp Thomas Browne, the administrative officer at Amersham police station who found Dr Davidson's body on 10 November, heard in recent years that a bus driver murdered the doctor. Did other members of the Chiltern Medical Society learn about this suspect at an exchange of confidential information during one of their regular meetings? Dr David Howell told me that one of the investigating police officers he knew well intimated he knew who had killed the doctor. Dr Bryn Neale, who lived three doors away from Kathleen Cook in Hyde Heath, said a police officer who was on the case suggested to him that he knew who had killed the doctor and that he [the killer] had committed suicide.

During the original police investigation nearly all patients with known psychiatric problems were checked. Did the police, having heard the doctor's evidence about George Garbett, in 1971, make further investigations about him? The doctor had, after all, got closer to the truth than anyone. Det Sgt Tony Dale, with one other police officer, called at the home of the bus driver to interview his widow. They took a softly-softly approach on the pretext of discussing her husband's suicide, making no mention of the new information that had come to light about her late husband's troubled mind or his involvement in the murder of Helen Davidson.

Dale said, 'It was all low-key. We couldn't tell her what we were really there for. And it would have been unkind to tell her. The search of his home produced absolutely no information to connect him with the enquiry.'

Having drawn a blank with Edna Garbett did the police continue their enquiries? Did any high-ranking police officers question Douglas and Pauline Willes about their live-in gardener and his movements on 9 November 1966? The couple had not been questioned during the original investigation five years earlier. This was a chance, the second time around, to obtain a few answers. Mrs Willes was aware Garbett had tried twice before to kill himself. But it would have been bad luck for her and her husband to discover a murderer, and one who was homosexual, had been living in their property for the last five years. A sordid scandal would be dreadful for the family. Undesirable publicity would have caused ripples in the village community and brought the family into disrepute. Police officers in those days knew they had to tread carefully with prominent members of society who were likely to complain about being harassed by the police. If the truth got out that Douglas Willes, a prominent London businessman who moved in upper-class circles, had housed a murderer, the publicity would be embarrassing. Did it make him exempt, though, from being questioned? I did wonder how much he knew about what had gone on under his nose at Well Cottage. Could it have been possible that the investigation was covered up?

Helen Davidson's murderer was dead. He had saved society the trouble of life imprisonment and saved his employers from the publicity of a murder trial. It seems quite coincidental that on Friday 23 July 1971, the day after delegates at the British Medical Association's annual conference voted unanimously to keep patients' private information secret, George Garbett, who had been consulting his doctor for some time, committed suicide.

Shortly after Garbett's suicide Mr and Mrs Willes moved to the Channel Islands.

14

Vicious Circle

A situation in which a problem causes other problems,
which in turn make the original problem worse.

By the beginning of January 1967 the investigation was over
for Det Ch Supt Jack Williams. It was a very short inquiry.
He went back briefly to Scotland Yard, disappointed he
had not been able to solve the murder. It would be his last
major investigation. The Metropolitan Police had relocated
to its new HQ: a twenty-storey office block at 10 Broadway,
Westminster. Increases in the size of the police force and
requirements of modern technology meant it had outgrown
its original site on Victoria Embankment adjacent to Canon
Row police station. Williams retired from the police force
three months later and promptly joined a firm of solicitors in Plaistow, East London that specialised in criminal
law. The task of finding Dr Davidson's killer was left to a
disillusioned Amersham police force under the guidance of
Det Insp Ernie Lund, Det Sgt Tony Dale and a couple of

detective constables. 'We made many visits to Hodgemoor Wood in the weeks after the murder,' said Dale, 'unsurprisingly we saw very few people there at all. The newspaper stories kept everyone away.' The weeks dragged on, they were no closer to cracking the case. In April 1967, satisfied there was nothing more to learn from the scene of the crime, Supt Aubrey Smith, the local divisional uniformed commander covering Amersham, Chesham, Beaconsfield and Gerrards Cross, gave written permission to the Forestry Commission to resume its work in Hodgemoor Wood. Ernie Lund retired after fifteen months leaving Tony Dale as the only survivor of the squad to follow up leads that came in.

In 2007, the Major Crime Review Unit at Thames Valley Police began looking at the murder of Helen Davidson. As previously mentioned, having no access to police archives from which to work, I wrote to the Chief Constable of Thames Valley Police asking if they could make available some background information on the case. Sara Thornton, the Chief Constable, responded 'as Helen Davidson's murder is a cold case they are not able to disclose information in accordance with an exemption under the Freedom of Information Act'.

Before Det Sgt Tony Dale retired from the police in 1986, he had been asked, as the older experienced detective sergeant with Amersham police, to periodically sift through and put in order all the old files stored in the garage 'archive' at Aylesbury police station, including that of Dr Davidson. Dale recalled:

I had to go through it because new leads might possibly come up in some important cases. There were a vast number of files that had accumulated at the rate of one drawer-full of a filing cabinet a year. They were all labelled 'Important files' with their date. Everything to do with Dr Davidson was up

there then … in a tea chest. I know it was there. Included
in it was a Pending Tray and all the odds and ends. I would
have known what was safe to throw away. I would use my
head as to which we should keep or not keep. I am told a
civilian took over the job of sorting through the old cases.
He wouldn't have known what was important. Whether he
kept the stuff as I would have done … an unsolved murder
must be kept. I would hope it's all still there.

Within a few weeks of that interview with Tony Dale in
2009, I uncovered new information regarding the evidence
from the case in 1966 that had been stored in the garage at
Aylesbury police station that Dale had described. I learnt
from a Buckinghamshire doctor, whom I cannot name, that
in 2007 two police officers from the Major Crime Review
Unit at Thames Valley Police visited him to ask about George
Garbett, the bus driver who had lived in Chalfont St Giles.
During their meeting the police officers told the doctor
that all exhibits from the Dr Davidson case, which had been
transferred to a shoebox awaiting periodic review (after Tony
Dale's retirement) disappeared sometime in 1986. There is no
evidence left.

This startling information made me reread a letter dated
8 May 2009 that I received from Sara Thornton, Chief
Constable of Thames Valley Police. It was written two years
after two of her cold case officers revealed to a third party that
all the Dr Davidson case evidence had been lost. She wrote, '[I]
would like to emphasise that all unresolved homicides within
the Thames Valley Police area remain "open" and are subject to
review. It is difficult to say what the likelihood is of solving the
case as it is determined by the strength of any new evidence
that is found.' Or lost, as the case may be, I thought to myself.

I wrote to Tony Dale about the new findings. He told me that he too had been visited by the same two police officers from the Major Crime Review Unit in 2007 (which he didn't mention when I met him) but said he was unaware of the disappearance of the Dr Davidson items. At the time of the visit by the police officers, Dale, who was the only surviving officer involved with the Dr Davidson investigation, had amassed his own archive of material about the case. I recall him saying at our meeting, in 2009, how I was too late and that if I'd come two months earlier I could have seen press cuttings and photographs in his files, including those pictures of Dr Davidson on the slab in the mortuary, and that he'd shredded it all a month earlier. I asked Dale which evidence in a 'shoebox' the two police officers would have been referring to when they called on my source, the doctor in Buckinghamshire. He said 'All the evidence from the case was more or less in the pending tray ... everything that was finalised as much as it could have been at that time. I tidied all the stuff and filed it. A civvy has thrown it away. That's what it means.'

The disappearance of the exhibits, from which something may have been learnt, occurred at the same time that the new DNA sampling technique was introduced in this country. Without that evidence therefore, there was no DNA. On what exactly were police officers in the Major Crime Review Unit hoping to base their case? I wrote another letter, dated 30 June 2009, to the Chief Constable of Thames Valley Police in which I said:

> Since receiving your letter [of 8 May 2009] I have spoken to a doctor in the Amersham area. He told me that two police officers (names supplied) from the Major Crime Review Unit who are looking at the case of Dr Helen Davidson's murder visited him in 2007. They told the doctor that there

is no evidence left in connection with the crime and that
it had been 'left in a shoe box and lost'. I must therefore ask
you if this is indeed the situation.

The Chief Constable did not reply to my letter.

At the time of the doctor's murder, DNA testing had not
been discovered. Would the new technology have helped find
the murderer? The Home Office's forensic pathologist, Dr
David Bowen, told me, 'I don't see why but I didn't know
much about the finer aspects of DNA.' Det Sgt Tony Dale, in
an interview with the *Buckinghamshire Advertiser* in November
2006 said he was not convinced there would be any useful
forensic evidence and 'because Dr Davidson was not sexually
assaulted I cannot imagine there would be any samples that
would be any good forty years on'. There may not have been
any suitable forensic evidence, but there is sufficient evidence
to show, quite simply, that the police in 1966 messed up this
murder investigation.

In 1966, a routine test that had been developed in the 1940s
called the Ouchterlony Test could have confirmed the origin
(human or animal) of the blood on the length of timber
assumed to be the murder weapon. As long as the wood had
been stored in reasonable conditions, had not been submerged
in water or exposed to extreme temperatures, the test would
have produced useful data. Other tests at the time could also
have confirmed that the blood on the alleged murder weapon
matched Dr Davidson's blood that had been spattered on surrounding trees and bushes, and on to her gloves, which were
encrusted with it. These tests were not carried out during the
police investigation.

Since its introduction in 1985, DNA fingerprinting has
been used to solve criminal cases all over the world. It is a

scientific process whereby samples of DNA are collected, collated and used to match other samples of DNA, which may have been found at the scene of a crime. The process is used as a means of identification when an attacker has left some kind of bodily fluid at a crime scene. In the case of Dr Davidson's murder it may have made a difference to the authenticity of the murder inquiry itself. The DNA technique could still have been used twenty years later to compare blood on the length of wood with samples of blood from Helen Davidson's gloves, to confirm that the wood found in the woodland really was the murder weapon as reported by the police.

Dr Davidson's blood-encrusted thick suede gloves, her binoculars, wedding ring, a signet ring she wore on her right hand and a brooch, all noted on Dr Bowen's preliminary examination of the body in the woods, would have been amongst many items stored in the police garage, which are now presumably lost. Other samples taken at the scene of the crime, on 10 November 1966 and later that day at the post-mortem included: dog hair control, rose hip, control head hair, raincoat, shoes, underwear and charcoal material from the wounds on her face. And what did happen to the doctor's wristwatch, which had been listed by Dr David Bowen during the preliminary examination at the crime scene but did not appear on the list at the time of the post-mortem? The watch would probably have stopped working when Dr Davidson hit the ground during the attack and would have contained evidence as to the precise time of her death, but it disappeared. Dr Bowen told me, 'In those days note taking was meticulous, the work was of a very high standard.' Was it, therefore, a case of sloppy policing in 1966, followed by insufficient care and attention in the mid-1980s that allowed the evidence to go missing? Something was not right.

There is evidence to show that the police adversely affected the outcome of the murder investigation because of their narrow-mindedness and flawed assumptions. Dr David Bowen examined Dr Davidson's body at 9.30 p.m., on 10 November 1966. In his secret post-mortem report, which he allowed me to read, I saw for myself how the police ignored evidence that did not fit their timings. Helen Davidson's death had been officially recorded as about 4 p.m. on Wednesday 9 November, just before it became dark. It appears that Dr Bowen had to estimate the time of death by taking into account conflicting and muddled circumstantial evidence from the police of when she was last seen. The police deduced that as sunset on 9 November was at 4.21 p.m., and as her body was found over three-quarters of a mile from her car in dense woodland, Helen Davidson must have set off on her walk no later than 3.30 p.m. when it was still light. Combined with casual police gossip about the doctor 'probably' heading up Gore Hill at about 3.15 p.m., this was the sum of the police estimation of timing. However, in Dr Bowen's handwritten notes at the bottom of the post-mortem report, which he wrote on 10 November 1966, he estimated the time of death to be between '4 p.m. and 10 p.m. approx. ... approx. 6 p.m.'. Surely the senior investigating officer, Det Ch Sup Jack Williams of Scotland Yard, whose business it was to investigate anything suspicious, would have seen a copy of Dr Bowen's post-mortem report. How did he miss the personal hand-written note from Dr Bowen at the bottom of the first page?

Dr David Howell had told me what he told the police in 1966: that he bumped into Helen Davidson, his practice partner, at 4 p.m. after afternoon surgery, outside the Old Bucks Library in Amersham on the Hill. Dr Howell said, 'It was just starting to be dusk. It was very peculiar that she went into the woods then.' The police ignored Dr Howell's testimony. Dr Davidson then drove another three miles to Hodgemoor Wood to go for a walk. What can now be assumed is that the doctor did not arrive at the lay-by close to Hodgemoor Wood until nearly 4.30 p.m., one hour after the police estimation, by which time it was getting dark. Dr Davidson was murdered much later than the police thought.

Instead of trying to make the story fit their theory on the timing of the murder using unsafe evidence, police investigators should have kept an open mind, asking themselves why the doctor chose to drive three miles from Amersham on the Hill and set off for a walk in dense woods as it was getting dark when there were other woods close by. Had the police not noticed it was unusual? It should have helped them build a picture of her character and an insight of what she was really like. There were clues, if the police had chosen to see them. Everything should have seemed important in a murder investigation.

Det Ch Supt Williams told the press that the doctor's binoculars probably caused her death. He deduced she had spied lovers conducting an illicit affair, was spotted, and one or both of them killed her, the killer making sure she 'wouldn't see again' by gouging out her eyes. But the binoculars round her neck were a red herring. Helen Davidson had actually come face to face with someone she knew in the woods. Dr Bowen was closer to the truth than the police when he told me Dr Davidson had obviously seen something that she shouldn't have seen, which was not quite the same thing as seeing lovers conducting an illicit affair.

Approximately seventy people said they had been walking in Hodgemoor Wood on the afternoon of 9 November. Oddly, nobody saw the doctor and no one saw anything suspicious.

The reason could simply have been because Helen Davidson was walking her dog an hour later than the other walkers who had already gone home because it was dark.

Referring to the length of burnt timber believed to be the murder weapon, Professor David Bowen stated in his biography *Body of Evidence* that 'the woodland in Hodgemoor Wood had been the subject of tree thinning and presumably some of the waste wood had been burnt'. But Bowen had been given insufficient and inaccurate information by the police who had jumped to conclusions about the source and significance of the length of wood. If they had kept up to date with local newspaper headlines they would have known that the Forestry Commission had been banned from felling, clearing, replanting and burning all trees in Hodgemoor Wood since the summer of 1966, pending reconsiderations of the future management plan for the woodland. With headlines like: 'The Battle of Hodgemoor Woods Begins', 'Splinters Fly over Hodgemoor Wood', 'Residents Angry about Plans for Hodgemoor Wood', 'Forestry Plan and Battle Reaches a Climax', police officers gathering intelligence about the murder in Hodgemoor Wood should have been alerted. Had they not noticed the press coverage?

From the start of my research I realised that the more you know about the victim, the closer you are to the murderer. The secret of Dr Davidson's death would most likely be found in the story of her life. As police officers working on the case at the Major Crime Review Unit at Thames Valley Police have no evidence to work from, bearing in mind everything has disappeared from the police garage in which it was stored, are they going back in history in search of clues in the suspect's and the victim's background? Have they moved away from the blinkered vision the police in 1966 held about the motiveless murder? Have they changed their perspective in order to solve the crime?

Helen Davidson was a private person who rarely socialised. Workplace colleagues knew very little about her or the kind of woman she was. Nearly all local doctors, who, following the introduction of the National Health Service in 1948, were members of the Chiltern Medical Society. But Dr Davidson, one of its founder members, was rarely seen at meetings. I believe she died, and the murder case was not solved, because of the private person that she was. If the police could have understood why she walked in the woodland late on that November afternoon in 1966, just as it was getting dark, they might have got closer to knowing the woman. Had the police learnt anything about their victim? Did they investigate if there was a personal element to her death? In 2003, ex-serving police officer with Buckinghamshire Constabulary, Len Woodley, published *Deadly Deeds: A Compilation of Buckinghamshire Murder Cases*. He devoted one chapter to the murder of Dr Davidson. In it, he wrote that 'the usual probing but discreet enquiries were made into the doctor's background, but these provided nothing tangible, as Dr Davidson led a blameless life devoted to the care of others'.

To me it was important to examine anything that happened to Helen Davidson in the months and years before she was murdered, which might have had a bearing on her demise. Why didn't the police delve deeper into her personal life about which nothing was really known? I had a gut feeling that the car crash in which the doctor was involved in 1961 – in which the young motorcyclist Michael Larcombe was left brain-damaged and in which her friend Brig John Cheney, the Chief Constable of Buckinghamshire, had taken an unusually keen personal interest and prosecuted in the case of careless driving brought against her – was in some way linked with the murder. This car crash, coupled with details of the old-boy network operating at the time, did provide an intriguing contrast to the previous, blemish-free characterisation of Dr Davidson. What on earth must this woman have felt like in those five years following the accident? Then, what if the incident that so few knew about should become generally known and raked over in public during the investigation into her murder? It would cause extreme embarrassment. But it was suitably covered up – an aspect of some of the policing then that left a nasty taste. It seems the police were putting the sensitivities of her family and colleagues before doing their job of asking awkward questions and solving the case. If the police had discovered the fugues that the doctor had developed as a result of the trauma of the accident, perhaps they would have been more open-minded about the timing of the murder. As an investigator there were inconsistencies that concerned me about the car crash. Was it a case of let sleeping dogs lie during the murder investigation?

The saga about the car crash surfaced again in the 1980s. This time the details were more confusing. It made me wonder who knew what, who was protecting whom and for what reason. It made me question again the transparency of the case of careless driving brought against the doctor. It made me wonder if the subsequent murder investigation was conducted with the same degree of concealed agendas.

Det Sgt Tony Dale is the only remaining Amersham police officer with any knowledge about Dr Davidson's car crash. He told me at our meeting about *the* motorcyclist involved in the crash who made occasional complaints to the Amersham police over a number of years. He gave the impression he had the full picture about it. But his knowledge was actually

limited, admitting to me he did not know that two motorcyclists were involved in the crash. He said:

> I really cannot remember the nature of the complaints
> from the motorcyclist but do recall they were somewhat
> rambling about Dr Davidson not being prosecuted. Then a
> letter arrived in the 1980s. This bloke was trying to resur-
> rect the case. He'd written to the chief superintendent who
> didn't know of the case, so it came to me, the only police
> officer left with any knowledge of the case, to answer it.
> I drafted the letter. I knew of it in a reasonable amount of
> detail. I certainly knew that Cheney had sent the file away
> to a solicitor for an opinion. A suitable reply was sent reiter-
> ating that the decision not to prosecute was based on advice
> from independent solicitors. Details were filed with the
> murder file at Aylesbury.

Reading between the lines I could see someone who, as sole
survivor of the Amersham police from the 1960s and who
knew some of the details about the car crash, may have uncon-
sciously converted observations into facts.

Michael Larcombe told me that he did not write any letters
to Amersham police about the car crash. It can only be assumed
therefore that Michael's friend Brian Woolsey, a talented artist,
potter and photographer but about whom I have found very
little personal information, must have written them. I did
discover that in the early hours of a July morning in 1993,
Brian Woolsey committed suicide in Newquay in Cornwall.
He was 53. He had spent some time in Bodmin Psychiatric
Hospital but was released in 1993 and moved into a residential
care home in Newquay for people with mental health problems.
He was there for just sixteen days before he took his own life.

The Davidson family, members of the upper class who mixed in aristocratic circles, would want their past history to remain secret. Helen's late uncle, Sir Nigel Davidson, was involved with the League of Nations mandate after the First World War through which Britain and France would rule the Middle East, and establish the state of Iraq. Helen's father, Alan Davidson, had been involved in the supply of ammunition to theatres of war in the First World War and was in personal contact with the Secretary of State for War. Surviving members of the family would not want an establishment scandal erupting, and their name brought into disrepute. Particularly as it was only three years since British spy Kim Philby's defection from the Middle East to Russia. Sir Nigel Davidson's close association in the Middle East with Kim Philby's father might be relevant. Did someone put the kibosh on the police investigation because of Helen Davidson's aristocratic connections? Were unsavoury details about the case, which could damage the doctor's family name and social circle, covered up? Were the police, who were not in the same class, out of their depth dealing with the secret lives of well-connected people?

Were the police also out of their depth dealing with members of Dr Davidson's own very private profession? And did the medical profession with its doctor–patient confidentiality principles contribute to her killer not being brought to justice? It certainly was a stumbling block. In July 1971, an article in *The Times* reported on the investigation of doctors' confidentiality principles at the British Medical Association's annual conference the previous day. It stated:

A sense of confidence between doctor and patient is essential to the practice of good medicine. It means that a patient should not be inhibited from consulting a doctor whenever the need arises or from speaking with complete freedom in such a consultation. Yet he can be expected to do so only if he can feel assured that whatever he says is for the doctor's ears alone. This is the basis of the principle of medical confidentiality.

Delegates at the BMA conference voted to keep patients' records confidential.

Should the doctor not have shared his information about George Garbett with Amersham police before the man committed suicide? A breach of confidentiality may have serious consequences for doctor-patient relationships, as well as for the doctor's reputation, and clearly he did not feel duty-bound to tip the police off about his suspicions. Wasn't this one of the occasions when one's obligation to the safety of others and the greater good must override one's duty of confidentiality to the patient, in this case the disclosure of a serious crime? There was sufficient reason for the police to arrest George Garbett. Instead the patient was able to take his life, thereby leaving the murder of Dr Helen Davidson unsolved for another forty-five years. Doctors apparently helped the police in their original enquiries five years earlier by checking patients with a grudge, those who had mental health problems or anything that could suggest Dr Davidson had an enemy. Seemingly the process at that time did not undermine patient-doctor confidentiality.

Len Woodley wrote in his book *Deadly Deeds*: 'Each year, as the anniversary of the slaying came round, the local press would send a reporter to interview Det Sgt Dale, who would obligingly take them to the murder scene in order that a photograph could be taken and a story published, with a view hopefully to jogging someone's memory.' Tony Dale

showed me a photocopy of an article that appeared in the
10 November 2006 edition of the *Bucks Free Press* to mark
the fortieth anniversary of the doctor's death. In it were photographs prominently positioned on the page, captioned:
'Unforgettable *Bucks Free Press* issues on the twentieth anniversary of the murder and on the thirtieth anniversary.' Dale
said: 'On each anniversary the press wanted to see the position
of the indentation of the doctor's head in the ground, where
her attacker had used a boot to grind it down.' Bearing in
mind the public passion for the unsolved murder and hoping
to prompt a response from the public, it was thought someone
would remember something. No one came forward. Strangely,
when I searched for these anniversary stories in the *Bucks Free
Press* the articles had disappeared. The archivist at the *Bucks
Free Press*, at its HQ in High Wycombe, wrote, 'You won't
believe this, and I find it difficult to believe it as well, but
I have searched bound copies and microfilms of the *Bucks Free
Press* issues in October/November 1986, 1996 and 2006 and
have found nothing.' The archivist at the Newspaper Library
in London told a similar story. Despite checking the first and
second editions of the paper for the relevant dates in 1986 and
1996 they were unable to find any mention of the Dr Helen
Davidson case. What was going on?

As I had received no help from Thames Valley Police, on
5 March 2012, I wrote to Det Ch Supt Hamish Campbell at
New Scotland Yard. He had recently taken over a new team
to tackle the number of murders that remain unsolved in
the capital. As Scotland Yard and a London forensic pathologist were called in to investigate the murder of Dr Davidson
in Buckinghamshire in 1966, I thought I might make a
breakthrough with Scotland Yard, having failed to receive
any assistance from Thames Valley Police. A fortnight later

I received a reply to my letter from a police officer in the Homicide and Serious Crime Command Special Casework Investigation Team at Scotland Yard:

> I write in response to your letter to Detective Chief Superintendent Campbell. I have searched our Records Management System and The National Archives and the Metropolitan do not hold the investigation files relating to Dr Helen Baker, née Davidson's murder. As you appreciate it is very difficult for us to comment on any unsolved murder, especially to non-related parties but without any available files we are not in a position to make any comment on the investigation. I have, however, contacted Peter Beirne of the Thames Valley Police Major Crime Review Team. He has confirmed the initial investigation was a joint one with the Met, who supplied the senior investigating officer but the file now remains with TVP. I have passed him a copy of your letter, at his request and he may be in touch with you. Thank you for your interest in this case.

Peter Beirne did not contact me.

★★★

Cold case: 'a crime that has remained unsolved for a long period of time, has no new evidence, and has been deemed a low priority by its original investigating agency or department.' From *The Concise Dictionary of Modern Medicine* by J.C. Segen.

Appendix

CHIEF CONSTABLE FINED

MOTORING OFFENCE

Brigadier J. N. Cheney, aged 60. of Grimms Hill, Great Missenden, Chief Constable of Buckinghamshire, at Great Missenden yesterday was fined £5 on a summons for driving a motor car without reasonable consideration for other road users. He had pleaded Guilty. His licence was also endorsed. and he was ordered to pay three guineas advocate's fee.

Mr. R. D. Sale, solicitor for the prosecution. said that on January 2 it was dark and drizzling. and when the Chief Constable was turning right, with his headlights dipped. a learner motor cyclist, approaching the car, slowed down, and turned across in front of the car. The motor cyclist mounted a pavement and came off. There was no impact between the car and the motor cycle. The motor cyclist had said his speed was not more than 20 or 30 m.p.h. at the time, and the car was well over on his (the motor cyclist's) side of the road.

Mr. J. F. Stevens, for the defence. said that there was no question of cutting across the path of an oncoming vehicle. The only possible criticism was that he traversed rather more of the initial turn than was reasonably considerate. His client came to the conclusion that if he had not been there and placed his car in that position in relation to the oncoming motor cyclist, the motor cyclist would not have been placed in a dilemma. and the accident. whatever the cause, would not have happened.

The Times, 13 March 1956.

Two Hurt In Road Crash

TWO young motor cyclists were seriously injured when they were involved in a collision with a car at the Stationroad junction at Amersham on Friday.

One of the motor cyclists. Michael Larcombe, an 18-years-old leather-driver. of "Copperkins", Copperkins-lane. Amersham. sustained severe head injuries. The other. Brian Woolsey, a 21-year-old student. who gave his address as care of the Roman Catholic Church. Amersham-road. Chesham Bois. fractured his left leg and foot.

The younger rider was taken to Amersham Hospital but was later transferred to High Wycombe Hospital, where both were detained.

The car was driven by Dr. Helen Davidson of "Ashlyn" North-road. Chesham Bois.

On Wednesday a spokesman at the hospital said that Larcombe. who sustained fractures of the skull and was still unconscious; was showing slight improvement, and that Woolsey was "comfortable".

Bucks Free Press, 7 July 1961.

Helen Davidson and Herbert Baker's marriage certificate.

Helen Davidson's birth certificate.

Helen Davidson's death certificate.

PRICE 5d.

Police believe killer is local man

IT is now five weeks since Dr. Helen Davidson's body was found in Hodgemoor Woods, and the murderer is still at large.

Detectives heading the hunt for the killer are convinced that he must be a local man who is being sheltered.

Det. Supt. Jack Williams, who is leading the hunt, feels sure that the murderer must have given himself away by strange behaviour but that his family are too loyal to him to give him up.

Closer net

The search is now concentrating more on Seer Green and Coleshill than on Amersham since they are nearer to the scene of the crime.

No fresh evidence has been forthcoming, and the police are now re-checking the 500-600 statements they took some time ago in the search for new clues to the identity of the killer.

POLICE SEEK LOVERS IN MURDERHUNT

POLICE hunting the killer of Dr. Helen Davidson are appealing for information about courting couples who visit any of the local woods.

They suspect that a married man might have murdered the 49-year-old Amersham doctor in the belief that she was an investigator watching the couple.

"We think it might have been an illicit courting couple," Supt. Jack Williams, of the Yard, said on Monday.

"It could well be that somebody thought that she was watching them, maybe for divorce proceedings or something, because it would appear they have gone to put her eyes out of action, and they appear to us to have stamped on her binoculars."

WEAPON

Dr. Davidson, a keen amateur ornithologist, generally carried a pair of binoculars with her whenever she went out for a walk.

"We would like to know — confidentially, of course — if anyone is aware of any couples going into the woods of an afternoon for illicit courtship," Supt. Williams explained.

"It may well be somebody is responsible who possibly cannot afford to be exposed."

This appeal follows the identification by the police of the weapon that was used — a piece of burnt wood about 2 ft. 6 in. to 3 ft. long, found lying near the murder scene.

CONFIDENCE

"That shows that whoever went up there didn't have a weapon," Supt. Williams said.

"I am beginning to think that the binoculars were the cause of her death.

"They may have thought that she was an inquiry agent."

Supt. Williams again emphasized that anyone who comes forward with information would be treated in the strictest confidence. He is prepared to meet them anywhere to discuss what they have to say.

Memorial donors to choose

THE Helen Davidson Memorial Fund committee has decided that donations will be used for either a medical or a religious memorial, according to the wishes of the donor.

Donations received by Barclays Bank, Amersham, for the fund will automatically go into the medical section of the fund —which will aid Amersham and Chesham hospitals.

But anyone wishing to contribute to the religious section —for some form of memorial at Hyde Heath church — has only to say so on his donation.

Mr. Herbert Baker, the murdered doctor's husband, is a member of the committee and a lay reader of Hyde Heath church.

Buckinghamshire Advertiser, 15 December 1966.

Buckinghamshire Advertiser, 1 December 1966.

Police hunt psychopath for Dr. Davidson's murder

KILLER BEHIND SOMEONE'S DOOR?

Faithful Fancy guards Mistress's dead body

Both doctor and a friend

FULL SCALE manhunt is being organized in Bucks this week following the discovery in Hodgemoor Wood, near Chalfont St. Giles, on Thursday of the brutally battered body of Dr. Helen Davidson. And police are pursuing a theory that someone in the area may be sheltering the killer.

"Somebody in the locality must have a good idea who this man is," Supt. Jack Williams, of Scotland Yard, said on Tuesday.

"I should think this is the type of man who may find it hard to keep it to himself.

"It is a dreadful thing for a man to have on his conscience. He may open up and tell somebody something in some pub or cafe."

Mr. Williams appealed to anyone who knows anything concerning the identity of the killer to come

have other stories concerning women volunteering to act as decoys.

An appeal has been issued for anyone who was walking

ham Bois, was found lying in woods about three quarters of a mile along Amersham-lane, near the main Amersham-Beaconsfield road.

Search

The search for her was carried out by police and troops from a nearby Army School of Education at Wilton Park, Beaconsfield, after her husband reported that she had not returned from a bird watching

DR. HELEN DAVIDSON had practised in the Amersham area for a number of years, and during that time she had become a well-known and liked personality.

When the police described her as "popular," they were not overstating the case.

"I've found her to be a wonderful doctor — in fact the best I have known," said one local man who has been one of Dr. Davidson's 3,500 patients for many years.

"Terrible deed

Buckinghamshire Advertiser.

---

t Circulation in the County   **5d.**

FOUL PLAY CANNOT BE RULED OUT—POLICE

Woman Doctor's Body Found In Hodgemoor Wood

A 54-YEARS-OLD Amersham doctor, Dr. Helen Davidson, was found dead with severe head injuries in Hodgemoor Wood, Chalfont St.-Giles, yesterday afternoon, following a 12-hour search in which more than 100 troops joined police and tracker dogs in combing the two square miles of woodland.

After the discovery of her body in a thicket, about a mile from the Amersham-Beaconsfield road, Superintendent Aubrey Smith, who led the search, told the 'Free Press': "Foul play cannot be ruled out."

Dr. Davidson, a keen amateur ornithologist, was last seen alive at 4 p.m. on Wednesday, when she left her home at "Ashlyn", North-road, Chesham Bois, with her six-years-old wire-haired terrier, "Fancy", to go bird watching in Hodgemoor Wood.

When she was found, lying on her back on a bed of leaves at about 2.30 p.m. yesterday, the dog was lying silent, but alive, across her legs.

THE SEARCH

The search was launched at 2 a.m. after friends, looking for her with her husband, Mr. Herbert Baker, found the doctor's blue Hillman car parked and locked on a lay-by off the Amersham-Beaconsfield road near the "Magpies" public house.

Troops from the Army Education Corps Headquarters at Wilton Park, Beaconsfield, were called in at about 11 a.m. to join about 40 policemen in searching the wood.

Dr. Davidson was married to Mr. Herbert Baker three years ago. She was in practice, under her maiden name in Amersham.

When she left home she was wearing a blue-grey jacket and skirt and was carrying a pair of binoculars.

Later yesterday two Scotland Yard detectives were called in and a Home Office pathologist went to the scene and examined the body.

DROP ANCHOR

A new boat as part of motel landscaping layout for mooring 50 to 100 boats at the Motel Site, Wraysbury-road, Wraysbury, it the intention of Mr. C. Davis, c/o Messrs. Kent and Turley, 6, Gray's Inn-road, London, W. C. 1 and application for planning permission has been made to Eton R. D. C.

DILEMMA

Two flats have been acquired by High Wycombe and District Hospital Management Committee in Station-road, Amersham, for married junior medical staff. The committee are hoping to acquire more flats in High Wycombe for medical staff.

Bucks Free Press,
11 November 1966.

Murder victim's husband makes an appeal

'DO NOT FEEL RESENTMENT'

HE ASKS CONGREGATION

THE CONGREGATION at Hyde Heath Church on Sunday heard an appeal from the husband of Dr. Helen Davidson, who was found murdered in woods near Amersham two days earlier. Dr. Davidson, who was known by her maiden name, died from head wounds. Her husband, Mr. Herbert Baker, is a Lay Reader. Preaching at the Remembrance Day service he asked the congregation not to feel resentment towards his wife's killer.

The church at Hyde Heath is a daughter church of Little Missenden Parish Church.

Mr. Baker took as his text: "Death where is thy sting, grave where is thy victory?"

He told the congregation: "I chose this text two months ago, but I little thought I would have to rely on these words so soon."

Mr. Baker said he knew the dark days would come when he would miss his dear wife terribly, and would be tempted to despair, but he knew his Saviour would not fail him.

Dr. Davidson was aged 49 and lived with her husband at Ashlyn, North Road, Chesham Bois. They were married in 1961.

Dr. Davidson was reported missing last Thursday when she failed to return from a bird-watching expedition.

DOG WITH HER

Hodgemoor Woods, near the road between Amersham and Beaconsfield, were searched by police and military personnel after Dr. Davidson's car was found in a lay-by. Her wire-haired terrier, "Fancy", was near the body.

On Tuesday Det. Supt. Jack Williams, of the Scotland Yard Murder Squad, who is investigating the murder, appealed to any friends or relatives who might be shielding the killer.

He said: "Don't shield this man. He needs help. No-one can come home after doing a thing like this and act normally."

Dr. Davidson had been in general practice in Chesham Bois for more than 20 years. She was Divisional Nursing Surgeon for the St. John Ambulance Brigade in the district, and had travelled a lot in the county as an external examiner for the Red Cross.

Ornithology was one of her main interests and she made many bird-watching trips into the country-side.

Dr. Davidson was buried in Little Missenden churchyard yesterday (Thursday), after a private service at Hyde Heath. After the burial a short service was held in Little

A wedding day picture of Dr. Helen Davidson and Mr. Herbert Baker.

Bucks Herald, 18 November 1966.

Herbert Baker with Helen Davidson's dog, Fancy, in *The Evening News*.

1st. Med. 9.B. 1938.

London (Royal Free Hospital) School of Medicine for Women

(UNIVERSITY OF LONDON.)

HUNTER STREET, BRUNSWICK SQUARE, W.C.1.

APPLICATION FOR ADMISSION.

I hereby apply to be admitted as a Student of the School, subject to the provisions of Art. 30* of the Articles of Association of the School, and I declare that I intend to pursue a complete course of qualifying medical study, and to present myself in due course to the Examining Boards with a view to obtaining a registrable diploma.

I undertake to conform in all respects to the regulations laid down by the Council, and in particular to abstain from presenting myself to any Examining Board until I have received from the Dean of the School full permission to do so.

Signature *Helen Davidson*

Address *14, Portinscale Rd, Putney. S.W.15.*

Date *30/5/34.*

TESTIMONIAL.

(To be signed, when possible, by a Teacher from the previous place of Education, or by someone in a recognised official position.)

I have known Helen Davidson

for the last 4 *years, and I recommend her for admission to the London (Royal Free Hospital) School of Medicine for Women.*

Signature H. V. Stuart

Address White Lodge, Sherborne

Date June 6th 1934

The Dean is authorised, in any case in which she may think it necessary, to require that this recommendation should be counter-signed by a Member of the Council.

*Article 30 is as follows:—"The Council shall have absolute discretion as to the admission of Students to the School, and full power to dismiss any Student attending the School or any Classes of the School, for any cause deemed by the Council sufficient."

SEE OVER.

PARTICULARS TO BE SUPPLIED BY STUDENT.

Full Name	Helen Davidson
Age. of date of Birth	16 yrs 8 months. October 1st 1917
Birthplace.	London.
Permanent Address.	14, Portinscale Road Putney S.W.15.
London Address (if other than above).	
Name & Address of Parent or Guardian or nearest relative	Alan J. Davidson Esq 14, Portinscale Road Putney. S.W. 15.
Previous places of Education including Schools and dates of attendance	Putney High School. May 1926 —Aug: 1930 Sherborne School for Girls Sept: 1930 — Aug: 1934.
Preliminary Arts Examination passed. Date.	School Certificate with matriculation. (7 credits) July 1933
Other Examinations passed, with dates.	Cambridge 1st M.B. Mechanics only. December 1933
Qualification desired	M.B.

Helen Davidson's application for admission to London School of Medicine for Women. (Royal Free Hospital Archives)

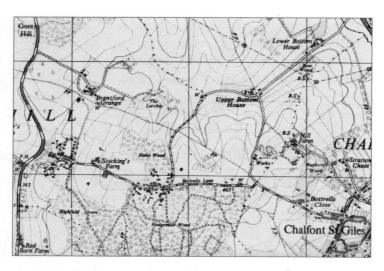

Gore Hill, Bottrells Lane and environs. (Reproduced from Ordnance Survey map, 1965)

A street map of Amersham in the 1960s. (G.I. Barnett & Son Ltd)

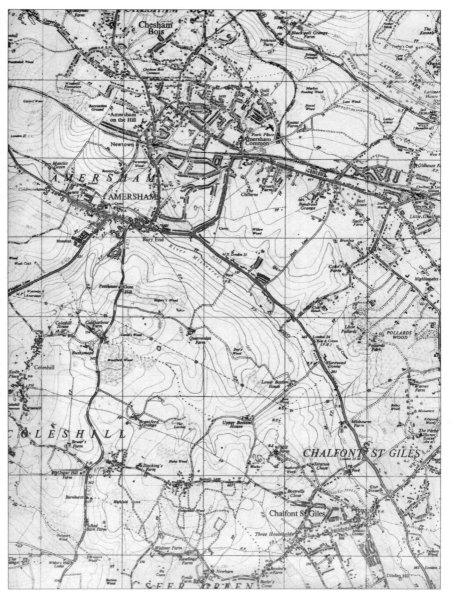

Chesham, Amersham, Chalfont St Giles overview. (Reproduced from Ordnance
Survey map, 1965)

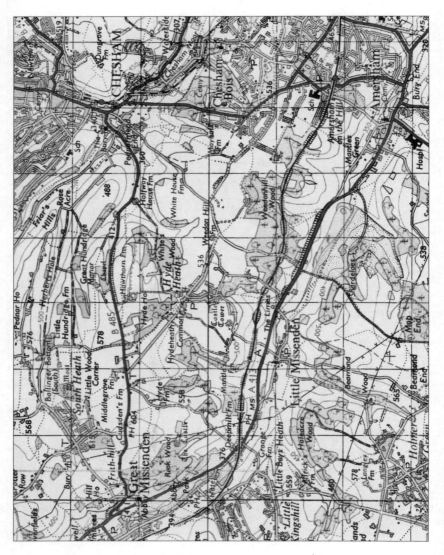

Chesham, Hyde Heath, The Missendens overview. (Reproduced from Ordnance
Survey map, 1965)

DEPARTMENT OF FORENSIC MEDICINE
CHARING CROSS HOSPITAL MEDICAL SCHOOL

Senior Lecturer
D. A. L. BOWEN,
M.A., M.B., B.Chir., M.R.C.P.(Ed.), D.Path., D.M.J.
M.C.Path.

82, CHANDOS PLACE,
LONDON, W.C.2.

Telephone No. TEMPLE BAR 7768 (Ext 222)

At 7.20p.m. on 10th November, 1966 I went with Det. Supt. Bowker, Det. Ch. Insp. Barrett and Det. Ch. Insp. Napier to a wood near Amersham, Bucks, half a mile from the nearest road and was shown the body of a woman lying on the undergrowth. She was on her back, fully clothed, no signs of interference of the underclothing. The left arm lay by her side, the hand bent slightly inwards, fingers proximating to the level of the hip. The right arm was extended, the forearm bending upwards at an angle of 45° from the trunk, the left leg was quite straight, and the right leg bent 25° at the hip and 45° at the knee.

Rigor mortis was fully established in the limbs, she was wearing a light raincoat, the front collar and sleeves patchily covered with blood stains, both gloves appeared to be more heavily blood stained. The strap of a pair of binoculars was around the neck, the binoculars themselves lying between the right side of the head and the shoulder, the eyepieces tucked into the shoulder, heavily blood stained.

The face was covered with blood with black "dirt like" material covering the left cheek and around the mouth, and extended downwards to the jaw in a series of fine smeared lines. The main wound consisted of a very deep laceration which had crushed the nose and upper cheek running below the left eyelid to the inner corner of the right eye, the depths of the wound extensively stained by dirt and debris. There was also a gaping laceration across the front of the forehead and a superficial one on the chin.

Blood stains extended upwards onto her hair and onto leaves immediately to the right of the body, and some further isolated staining was seen at a distance of 3' from the head.

At 9.45p.m. the same evening I went to Amersham General hospital where I carried out a post mortem on the body which was identified to me by Sgt. Tale and Det. Con. Childerley as being that of Doctor Helen DAVIDSON / BAKER, aged 54.

Helen Davidson post-mortem. (Professor David Bowen)

POST MORTEM EXAMINATION

Helen DAVIDSON / BAKER   aged 54   FBY 73

at Amersham General Hospital Mortuary, on 10.11.66   at 9.45p.m.

Officers Present at the post mortem were:

Det. Supt. Williams, Central Office, N.S.Y.
Det. Supt. Bowker, Bucks.
Det. Ch. Insp. Barrett, Bucks.
Det. Ch. Insp. Napier, Met. Laboratories.
Det. Insp. Lund, Bucks.
Det. Insp. White, Bucks,
Det. Sgt. Woods, N.S.Y.
Det. Sgt. Baker, Bucks, Exhibits Officer.
Det. Sgt. Gaunt   )
Det. Con. Bailey   )   Photographers.

Clothing was removed in the following order: a pair of brown
suede gloves, fur lined; a wristlet watch; brown shoes;
a terylene rain coat with dog lead in left hand pocket; brown
woollen pullover; a patterned lined skirt; a handkerchief in
right sleeve; brooch on patterned shirt; white full length
slip; pink knickers; white girdle; vest and stockings; white
brassiere.   There was a ring on the right little finger and a
wedding ring on the left ring finger.

External Appearances:
              5' 7" in height, and 9 - 10 stone in weight.
Hypostasis was fixed along the back of the body and the liver
temperature was 61°F. at 10.25 p.m.   There was no sign of the
clothing being disarranged.

[handwritten annotations:] 37°c. / ie. 15hrs before / or 37°mm / ÷ 130°c   above RS above / tne. 4pm-10 pm. appaent / about b.t

Helen Davidson post-mortem. (Professor David Bowen)

Helen Davidson /Baker   FBF 73

The wounds on the face consisted of:

      1. An laceration 2" long, gaping to ½" with heavily abraded edges across the middle of the forehead.

      2. Laceration running right across the left eyelid curving downwards around its lower margin with bruising of the superficial tissues and a very superficial laceration immediately beneath the eyelid, the eye itself having prolapsed into the skull, following extensive fracture of the orbit.

      3. Main facial laceration 4½" long from a point an inch in front of the left ear running across the upper cheek to the base of the nose which was completely torn from the underlying tissues and then upwards to the inner margin of the right eyebrow. In the depths of this wound fragments of nasal, cheek and orbital bone were found penetrating to a depth of 1½" and reaching the nasal sinuses and base of skull.

      4. 1" long laceration along the lower margin of the left lower lip with abrasion extending laterally around it.

      5. Superficial 1" laceration on the left side of the chin with penetration to the bone.

      6. On the right side of the chin fine abrasions with four superficial abraded lacerations, and on the right cheek abrasions and a punctured laceration 1" in front of the right ear, ½" across. Also fine abrasions on the front of the neck, and on the left shoulder.

      7. Superficial lacerations along the lower margin of the right eyelid, ½" long, with ." long smaller laceration on either side of the eye with superficial bruising around it.

      8. 1" dried abrasion on left side of the neck with stippled abrasion just above it.

There was some superficial dirt staining on the lower legs.

The margins of all the wounds were stained by black debris.

Internal Examination:
   Skeletal System:

Reflexion of the scalp tissues revealed heavy bruising along the left side and front, particularly in the temporal region.

Fractures of nasal, cheek and orbital plate with extension through to the base of the skull close to the midline on the left side. The upper jaw was quite loose due to extensive fracturing and separation from the base of the skull. Lower jaw intact but loosened from its joint on the left side. Path of bruising above inner angle of the right collar bone.

Helen Davidson post-mortem. (Professor David Bowen)

Helen Davidson/Baker   FBF 73

Central Nervous System:
The brain coverings were healthy and some blood stained fluid was seen around the base of the brain, the surface and substance of which showed no sign of bruising.

Cardiovascular System:
The heart was of normal size and shape, containing some fluid blood, there was no valvular disease and the aorta and coronary arteries were perfectly healthy.   The heart muscle was normal, and the heart weighed 220g.

Respiratory System:
Some haemorrhagic spots were seen around the back of the voice box, but there was no sign of bruising, the air passages containing some blood stained fluid which had not reached the lung substance.   There was no natural disease.

Alimentary System:
The liver was pale, the gall bladder empty. The stomach was half full of food debris and a little fresh blood was also present, the lining being normal.   Pancreas and other organs healthy.

Uro-genital System:
The kidneys were of normal size and shape, some pallor present.   Uterus normal, bladder empty.

Spleen:
Small.

Endocrines:
Normal.

Conclusions:
This woman was quite healthy.   The injuries she had received were confined to the face and comprised one large laceration splitting open the left side of the face, and up to half a dozen smaller wounds, the latter being in keeping with multiple blows from a shod foot.

CAUSE OF DEATH: 1a.   HAEMORRHAGE

due to b.   FRACTURE OF THE SKULL

Dr. D.A.L. Bowen

Helen Davidson post–mortem. (Professor David Bowen)

Opposite: Letter and list from Det Ch Insp A. Napier to Dr D.A.L. Bowen.
(Professor David Bowen)

Metropolitan Police Forensic Science Laboratory

Please address any reply to THE DIRECTOR, and quote:—	2 *Richbell Place*, *Holborn, W.C.1*

Tel.: HOLborn 3801

16th November, 1966.

Dr. D.A.L. Bowen,
Dept. of Forensic Medicine,
Charing X Hosp. Medical School,
62 Chandos Place,
W.C.2.

Re murder of Helen Baker, Hedgemoor
Woods. Bucks. on 10th Nov.66.

    Attached is a list of the exhibits taken
possession of at scene, and at post mortem
examination on 10th November, 1966, respecting
the above case.

    Incidentally the large piece of burnt wood
found at the scene gives a strong reaction for
blood, and examination is being made to try and
identify the pieces of charcoal found in the
wound with this piece of wood.   Perhaps you
would like to see if sometime?   If you would
like to telephone me I will make the arrangements
for you.

(A. Napier)
Det. Ch. Insp. Lab.

Ext. 28.

List of samples taken at scene (Hedgemoor Wood) and post mortem
examination, 10th November, 1966.

Scene

    Dog hair control
    Rose hip

Post Mortem Amersham General Hospital

    Material from wounds ? charcoal
    Binoculars
    Left glove
    Right glove
    Raincoat
    Left shoe
    Right shoe
    Sweater
    Skirt
    Blouse
    Handkerchief
    Left stocking
    Right stocking
    Slip
    Knickers
    Roll on
    Vest
    Bra
2 vaginal swabs
    Anal swab
    Control head hair
    Control blood
    Stomach contents
    Debris from under sheet

THAMES VALLEY
POLICE

Sara Thornton QPM
CHIEF CONSTABLE

Thames Valley Police Headquarters
Kidlington
Oxon OX5 2NX

Tel: **(01865) 846002**
Fax: (01865) 846057

ST/EA/letters/2009/ Weller

8 May 2009

Ms Monica Weller

Dear Ms Weller

I refer to your letter dated of 29 April. The case of Dr Davidson is one of several that are the subject of investigation by the Major Crime Review Team. I am not at liberty to tell you the level of investigation but would like to emphasise that all unresolved homicides within the Thames Valley Police area remain 'open' and are the subject of review. It is difficult to say what the likelihood is of solving the case as it is determined by the strength of any new evidence that is found.

I understand that our perceived non co-operation may frustrate you in your desire to publish the story of Dr Davidson's death. However, in any request of this nature we have to ask "How will the disclosure of this information assist in the investigation" balanced against any distress that the publication may cause any living relatives or friends of the victim.

Taking this into account I do not believe that further disclosure would benefit our investigation and that is why your request for further information has been declined.

Yours sincerely

Sara Thornton

Sara Thornton
Chief Constable

Letter from the Chief Constable of Thames Valley Police, 8 May 2009.

TOTAL POLICING

Specialist Crime and Operations

Ms M Weller

SCD1 - Homicide and Serious Crime Command
Special Casework Investigation Team

Room 332
New Scotland Yard
10 Broadway
London
SW1H 0BG

Telephone: 020 7230 4294

Email: Susan.Farmer@met.police.uk
www.met.police.uk

Your ref: Unsolved Murders

21 March 2012

Dear Ms Weller,

I write in response to your letter to Detective Chief Superintendent Campbell. I have searched our Records Management System and The National Archives and the Metropolitan do not hold the investigation files relating to Dr Helen Baker, nee Davidson's murder.
As you appreciate it is very difficult for us to comment on any unsolved murder, especially to non-related parties but without any available files we are not in a position to make any comment on the investigation.

I have however, contacted Peter Beirne of the Thames Valley Police Major Crime Review Team. He has confirmed the initial investigation was a joint one with the MET, who supplied the Senior Investigating Officer but the file now remains with TVP. I have passed him a copy of your letter, at his request and he may be in touch with you.

Thank you for your interest in this case.

Yours sincerely,

A/Detective Inspector Susan Farmer

Letter from the Metropolitan Police, 21 March 2012.

Index

The History Press

The destination for history
www.thehistorypress.co.uk